CW01668468

He who knows only his own side of the case knows little of that. His reasons may be good, and no one may have been able to refute them. But if he is equally unable to refute the reasons on the opposite side, if he does not so much as know what they are, he has no ground for preferring either opinion.

John Stuart Mill

The Mistress of Novices and the Mistress of Postulants have been helping me by expressing opposite points of view.

The Sound of Music

ISBN 978-1-8381543-0-1

First paperback edition August 2020

Published by Debating For Everyone

www.debatingforeveryone.com

About the author

Julian Bell has worked as an English teacher for over thirty years, and since 2000 has been Head of English and Debating at Godolphin and Latymer School in London. When he arrived, Godolphin and Latymer had no debating provision whatsoever, but is now described as 'a flagship debating school'. As well as running Godolphin and Latymer's internal debating programme, which involves over 100 students, he is also founder and leader of three major debating competitions: the London Junior Debating League for Years 7-8, the London Middle School Debating Competition for Years 9-11, and the London Sixth Form Debating Competition for Years 12-13. He works as an oracy trainer and debate judge for both the English Speaking Union and The Noisy Classroom, and regularly visits schools across the country to offer consultancy and CPD for teachers and training for students in debating and public speaking.

To find out more, and to contact Julian Bell, visit his website:

Debating for Everyone

www.debatingforeveryone.com

CONTENTS

Welcome to The Debating Book!

This book is for you if:

- You have never done debating before and would like to start.
- You have only just started debating and you would like to get better.
- You are an experienced debater and you want to be the best you can be.
- You are a teacher who would like to set up debating in your school and you aren't sure what to do.
- You are an experienced debating coach and you would like to support your students even better.
- You are the parent of someone who does, or would like to do, debating, and you want to support them.

In this book, you will find all you need to know about debating. Read it carefully, and you will become a (much) better debater / debating coach.

In this book, you will be learning about: why you should do debating; how debating works; the basic skills of debating; bad arguments to avoid (and how to attack them when other people use them), and good arguments to persuade people; the big issues and ideas that debates are about; useful facts about the world that debaters need to know; tricks to make your speeches more persuasive; how you can use debating in lessons; and how to set up and run debating in your school. You will also find a full transcript of an expert debate with close analysis, explaining what star debaters do and how they do it.

You can read this book by yourself; take it to debating competitions for reference; use it as a textbook for debating training sessions. You can dip in and out of different chapters as you need to.

I hope I've persuaded you to read this book! (Debating is all about persuading people.)

If so, read on …

CHAPTER 1

Why do debating?

In this chapter we're going to learn why you should do debating.

I'm going to persuade you (because debating is all about persuading) that debating is one of the best things you can do. It's a chapter which, like debating, is full of becauses.

So.

You're going to stand up in front of a room full of people you don't know - or, worse, a room full of people you do know - and say a lot of things you don't believe in. Then the people sitting opposite you are going to tell you why everything you just said is wrong. They're going to find fault with every word that just came out of your mouth. And, when it's all over, someone else is going to tell you what you did wrong and why the people sitting opposite you are better than you. In other words, you're going to be a debater.

Why would you want to do that?

Here are seven answers to that question:

1. **Because you do debating all the time anyway.**
2. **Because debating will make you more confident.**
3. **Because debating will help you to do better at school.**
4. **Because debating will make you lots of friends.**
5. **Because debating will help you to understand other people better.**
6. **Because debating will help you to understand the world better.**
7. **Because debating will save the world.**

Convinced yet? No, I didn't think so.

In true debating style I now have to make my case. I have to give reasons for my *becauses*.

Here goes...

1 Because you do it all the time anyway

Debating is one of the most basic of human activities

Think you aren't a debater? Think again.

You probably started being a debater when you were about four. When your Mum told you to put your shoes away in the cupboard, and you said, 'why?' And she said because it will keep the house tidy and stop your shoes getting lost, and you said, 'But if I leave them out by the door I can put them on quicker when I leave the house.' See what you and your Mum did back then? She made a proposition. You questioned it. She came back with arguments. You came back with counter-arguments. That's debating. You probably didn't win that debate. But at least you were getting started.

Or when, in the playground, you wanted to play one game and your friends wanted to play another, and you dug your heels in and said, 'We're going to play my game', and they said 'why?' and you gave them reasons, and answered their objections, until they gave in. You were debating then.

Or when your brother or sister wanted to use the computer to play a game and you needed to do your homework on it, or you wanted to play a game and they needed to do their homework, and you gave them reason after reason until they gave in. You were debating then.

Or when you wanted to go to a party and your parents said no and three hours of persuading later they said yes. You were debating then.

Or even when you lay in bed all night, not able to sleep, trying to decide whether or not you should drop History, or whether or not you should forgive your friend, or whether or not you should ask that person out, or whether or not you believed in God, or whether or not you should ever wear those trousers again, and the argument in your head kept going backwards and forwards until, just as the birds started singing, you knew what the right thing to do was. You were debating then (just with yourself).

Debating is one of the most basic of human activities.

Everyone does it, in every culture, and they always have done and they always will do. It happens because humans have choice. It happens when there is more than one course of action, or more than one way of interpreting a situation, or more than one way of seeing the world. It involves putting each side of the case in turn, and letting each side in turn be looked at and questioned and pushed and prodded and kicked, until one side comes out stronger, and the decision can be made, and we see the world in a different way. We all do it, all the time. What we call 'debating', the activity that takes place in clubs and competitions in schools, is just a formalised, disciplined way of doing what everyone does all the time - only doing it better.

Debating is a way of using your mind, a way of thinking.

We all have minds, of course. We all think. We also all have bodies, and we all move them. Athletes have bodies, and they move them too. The difference is that athletes train their bodies and discipline them until they can move them faster, stronger, further. Debating is like athletics for the mind. It trains you to think faster, stronger, further.

2 Because it will make you more confident

Do you remember the first time you had to speak in public? Or the second? Or the third?

How did you feel?

Were your legs shaking? Did your face (and / or other parts of your body) go red? Was your stomach like a hamster who's just drunk a triple espresso running on her wheel? Did you think everyone was laughing at you?

Everyone feels like that. Even people who seem utterly confident fear failure and humiliation, whether they're doing 'Show and Tell' in Year 1, or presenting on a topic in class, or doing a reading in Assembly, or making their first speech in the House of Commons, or giving their inaugural address as the newly elected President of the United States. I have no evidence for this, but I bet Martin Luther King went to the bathroom more often than usual just before he gave his 'I have a dream' speech.

It never goes away.

So what should you do about it? Hide under the duvet? Or in the cupboard? Draw the curtains? Never go out?

That won't work.

Even if you don't become an MP, or President of the United States, or lead a mass movement against racism, you will have to speak in public, whatever line of work or way of life you end up in. You may well have to do it in your private life too. So you might as well get good at it.

Debating trains you to think faster, stronger, further

It never goes away, that adrenaline overload, that 'fight or flight' feeling. But it does get easier to manage. Here's how to manage it.

Back to athletes. They tend to be fitter than other people. How do they get fit?

Did you ever hear someone say, 'I can't go for a run. I'm not fit enough.'? That's an easy argument to demolish. Going for a run is how you get fit. Olympic gold medal winners weren't born fit; they got fit. And they got fit by running, or jumping, or throwing, again and again and again. Public speaking (which is to debating what running, jumping and throwing are to athletics) is no different. You get better at it by doing it. And the more you do it the more confident you will be, not least because you will have done it in the past and therefore know you can do it in the future. Athletes talk about 'muscle memory', the way in which, if you repeat a certain action often enough, it becomes automatic, almost a part of you. Your mind can develop muscle memory too. Speak in public often enough, and it will end up seeming as normal as speaking in private. Like anything else, the more you do it, the easier it gets. Debating will have you doing it a lot.

Like anything, the more you do it, the easier it gets

And there's more.

Public speaking isn't the only thing that debating will give you confidence with. It will also give you confidence with private speaking. I mean the sort of private speaking where someone wants you to do something, or think something, or even be something which you know in your heart of hearts is wrong - wrong for you, or maybe just wrong full stop. If you're not used to seeing the flaws in the other person's ideas, or defending your own way of thinking, then it can be hard to stand up for yourself. You can end up either giving in, or losing your temper and storming off, maybe losing a friend in the process. If you're a debater, though, you will be able to question what you've been told, and then put your side of the story calmly, confidently and assertively.

Debaters are the sort of people who can say what needs to be said without fear or anxiety, but also without having to bully or shout, both in public and in private. People respect them for it.

As one of my students said once:

'Since I've been a debater my parents tell me I've become much more argumentative. That is so not true!'

3 Because it will help you to do better at school

When I was at school, 90% of lessons consisted of us sitting there listening to a teacher who told us stuff which we wrote down. If we were lucky, he could keep good enough order for us to hear it all, and if we were even luckier, he made it interesting. Then, when we'd written it down, we learnt it off by heart, and wrote it all out again in an exam. The more we managed to remember, the higher a grade we got. The only time I got to express my views - the only time, almost, apart from break times and lunch times, I got to speak - was in the debating club.

It's different now. Students are encouraged to take much more part in their learning, to be much more active, to work collaboratively, to engage in discussion. However, there's still material to be covered, syllabuses to be completed, exams to prepare for. It can feel (back to hamsters) a bit like being on a treadmill.

Here's where the debating club comes to the rescue (again). None of the stuff you talk about in debating club will ever be in an exam. You're free to try and to fail, to get things right and get things wrong, and your future doesn't depend on it. You don't have to remember any of it once the debate's over.

And yet, at the same time, debating club will send you back to your lessons better prepared to succeed in them.

Why?

What we call humanities subjects - English, History, Geography, Philosophy and Religion, Classics, and so on - all require you to build arguments step by step, supported by evidence, taking nothing for granted. That's what debating does too. A lot of the issues you will discuss in those subjects - big topics about what's right and wrong, about how the world should be run, about what we can and can't know - come up in debating. And don't forget languages, and Maths and science subjects. They require you to think logically and clearly, to go from one concept to another in a methodical way: so does debating.

So, when you come out of debating club and go back to your lessons, you'll find that your subjects will make more sense, that you will know more about them, that you will be more confident in expressing your views in them, and that your essays will be clearer, better planned and better argued. I'm an English teacher, and I can always tell which of my students do debating, from the clarity and rigour of their writing. Debating is not only great fun, it also makes you smarter at school.

Debating is not only great fun, it also makes you smarter at school

4 Because it will make you lots of friends

Now there's a funny idea. Arguing with people helps you to make friends with them? How does that work?

Debaters are fun to be around

Here's how.

A little known fact about debating is that it is a team activity. You do it in a team of two, or sometimes three. That's a small team, but it's still a team. There is nothing more intense, more bonding, than working under pressure as a team; supporting each other, helping each other, respecting each other, balancing your weaknesses with your team mate's strengths, her strengths with your weaknesses. When you have fifteen minutes to prepare to speak to a crowded room on a topic you know hardly anything about, that's when you find out if you can rely on someone. When what you're saying is interrupted every thirty seconds by someone telling you you're wrong, that's when you know who your friends are. And they will become friends, your team mates, because you will have been through that experience together.

Not just your team mates. If you're lucky, your school will have a debating club with many members, who get together on a regular basis to talk and argue and set the world to rights. You'll meet people from other year groups, other backgrounds, other political opinions, other faiths. You won't always agree. Arguments may get very passionate. One of my students got so excited in a debate that she suddenly started talking in French without even realising she was doing it (her parents were French speaking). You'll give as good as you get, but it will all be done in an atmosphere of mutual respect and courtesy. You'll get to know each other very well. You may well become life long friends.

If you take debating further, you may go on a residential course or debating competition where you'll meet people from other schools and other parts of the country. You'll spend all day (and quite possibly much of the night) arguing with each other, and you'll love it. One of my students told me that a weekend debating competition she took part in at the other end of the country was the best weekend of her life. I didn't inquire too closely into what she got up too, but I imagine it involved making friends. I have seen debating romances blossom at some of these events (what happens when they have their first argument?).

So of course debaters have lots of friends. Why wouldn't they? They're lively, intelligent people who love sharing their ideas with each other, and love listening to other people's ideas. They're fun to be around.

5 Because debating will help you to understand other people better

June 24th 2016 was one of the most extraordinary days of my life.

It was the day after the referendum in which Britain voted to leave the European Union, but it actually felt more like the day after some horrific terrorist attack.

In my first lesson, a student walked into the room, slammed her folder down on the table and said, 'Mr Bell, I am so angry!' As her friends arrived, they all got angry together. And angrier. And angrier. We were supposed to be studying the poetry of Wordsworth, but Wordsworth got pushed to one side, as they would talk about nothing else but the referendum vote. They told me about their parents crying at breakfast, worried about what would happen to their children. They told me about their fears for their future. They told me that they couldn't believe what had happened. How could they have done this? How could they have been so ignorant? How could they have been so stupid?

It went on like that all day. In my lessons. In the staff room. On the Tube. Talking to the neighbours. Talking to my family. Everyone, everywhere, looked like someone had just died. No, not just someone: hundreds of people; maybe thousands; maybe millions. One member of my family, who is the kindest, gentlest, most tolerant person I know, texted me to say: 'A victory for ignorance and stupidity.'

If everyone thought leaving the European Union was such a stupid idea, why did Leave win the referendum?

Because not everyone thought that. A lot of people thought leaving the European Union was a very good idea. 17.4 million of them, to be precise. The trouble was, neither I, nor my students, nor my colleagues, nor my friends, nor my family, nor the people I sat next to on the Tube, knew any of them. Or if we did, those people were keeping very, very quiet on June 24th 2016.

I teach in an independent school in London, the most cosmopolitan city in the world. Almost without exception, my students go on to Higher Education, and many of their parents went to university too. Some are from international families – often from the EU - and the majority can afford holidays abroad and are well travelled.

I went to university. My wife went to university. All our friends went to university (we met most of them at university). We travel a lot, because we can afford to.

If everyone thought leaving the European Union was such a stupid idea, why did Leave win the referendum?

Of course we all voted Remain. Why wouldn't we?

We (by we, I mean all the people I know) like to think that we voted for the EU because we're open-minded, tolerant, liberal people who welcome diversity, co-operation and sharing. What we don't like to think is that we voted for the EU because it suits our own interests.

What has this got to do with debating?

Quite a lot, actually.

In all the conversations I had about the EU referendum, and in all the conversations I overheard about the EU referendum, I never once heard anyone make the case for leaving the EU. All I heard was a kind of frantic competition to be the most worried (before the result) or upset (after the result) at the prospect of leaving the EU, and to be the most outraged at the ignorance and stupidity of Leave voters.

With one exception.

The Monday before the vote, I ran an assembly in which I staged a debate on the EU. Students had to listen to a speech for Remain, and a speech for Leave, given equal time. This wasn't without difficulties. The student who spoke for Leave was being given a hard time in the sixth form common room. People told her that she shouldn't be doing it; people were refusing to talk to her. I had to intervene on her behalf, to tell other students that this wasn't acceptable. When she gave her speech, though, it was much the more persuasive of the two. If I had been judging the debate, she would have won hands down. She didn't make me vote Leave, but she certainly earned my respect.

After the debate, we had a vote, by secret ballot. The result was 87% for Remain. Where did the 13% for Leave come from? Did they misread the ballot paper? Or were they, perhaps, persuaded by that student's speech? Whoever they were, they were keeping very quiet on June 24th.

But at least that debate forced the school, just for ten minutes, to listen to someone who did not see the world the way they saw it. And debating does that all the time. In a debate, whatever you say will be challenged, often very vigorously, and you will have to defend yourself. Debating means you can take nothing for granted. And there's more. Because you don't get to choose your side of the motion, you will often have to argue for something you don't agree with. If you are going to do that successfully, you have to enter into the mind of someone else, someone who sees the world

That debate forced the school, just for ten minutes, to listen to someone who did not see the world the way they saw it

in a completely different way from you, and, just for a moment, see things as they do. Even if you are arguing for something you believe in, you have to enter into the other side's way of thinking in order to better challenge it.

In debates, I've seen students from Israeli families argue for the Palestinian cause; I've seen devout Catholics argue for abortion rights; I've seen gay students argue against same-sex marriage. They may not have changed their minds at the end of it, but at least they came away understanding the people they disagreed with a bit better.

I've seen gay students argue against same-sex marriage

How could they have done this? How could they have been so ignorant and stupid? That was what I heard again and again in the days and weeks after the EU referendum. But who are this 'they'? They're our fellow citizens, that's who. The people we share our country with. They're not a tiny lunatic fringe. There are 17.4 million of them. They're not ignorant. They're not stupid. They just see the world differently from me, and the people I know. Whatever the future holds for Britain and the EU (and I have no idea what the situation will be by the time you read this book), we're still going to have to live together, to get along together, to share our country. If we make the effort to understand each other, it's going to be a much better country to live in.

Debating makes you understand other people. It builds up the understanding muscle in your mind.

Have a conversation with someone in which you argue for something you don't believe in. See how you feel at the end of it. Did anything change?

6 Because debating will make you understand the world better.

You have fifteen minutes to prepare for a debate. (Fifteen minutes, incidentally, in which you are forcibly separated from your phone, iPad or other device).

After that fifteen minutes, you're going to have to stand up and talk to the whole room about Brexit, or Trump, or climate change, or the gender pay gap - or whatever is in the news by the time you read this book, and therefore likely to be in a debating motion. Sitting opposite you are people who are going to try to prove you wrong. One way they can do this is by showing you've got your facts wrong. If you think Brexit is a brand of cereal, Trump is a character in a comedy programme, climate change means the difference between summer and winter and the gender pay gap is a geological phenomenon, then you're going to be in trouble. Even if you know a bit more than that, you're going to need to know more than the other side if you want to win the debate.

You need to read something longer than a Twitter post

How are you going to do that?

You need to get into habits. The habit of watching, reading, listening to the news. The habit, too, of being careful with what you read, of judging how accurate it is, of how much bias there is in it, of noticing what it chooses to put in and what it chooses to leave out. The habit of reading something longer than a Twitter post or an Instagram meme. The habit of being willing to listen to versions of current events you don't agree with (because one day you might have to argue for them). The habit of taking an interest both in the small details of the news and in the wider issues and forces behind them. The habit of working out why things happen as well as knowing what happens.

If you do all that, you will be well prepared for whatever motion you're given, whatever side you have to take.

But there's more (as there often is with debating).

If you do all that, if you really get to know the world around you and what's going on in it, you'll not only be a better debater, fully equipped with the facts and figures at her fingertips; you'll also be a better person. You'll be a fully engaged citizen of the world, who takes an interest in what is happening in it. The world can be a scary place sometimes. It can feel like a lot of bad things are happening, and they're out of our control. But knowing more about it, knowing why those things happen, gives you much more control than if you keep yourself in the dark. You'll be in a better position to influence what happens in that world. One day you may be able to change it for the better. One day you may even be able to save it.

Which brings us on to our last because.

7 Because debating can save the world

Imagine two friends, Alex and Ayesha.

They really like each other. They enjoy each other's company. They do lots of stuff together. Then, one day, Alex says or does something that Ayesha doesn't like. Ayesha feels hurt and let down by Alex. She feels angry about what has happened. So angry, that when she tells Alex about it, she finds herself raising her voice. But Alex doesn't seem to be listening. So she raises her voice some more. After a while she is shouting at Alex, and he feels threatened, even a little scared. So scared that he can't listen to what Ayesha is really saying. Instead of listening to what she's saying, he starts shouting back. Now Ayesha gets even more upset. She shouts even louder. She brings in stuff that has nothing to do with whatever originally upset her (why, exactly, did you tell Rebecca what my sister told me about her boyfriend? I told you not to tell anyone). So Alex retaliates, with more stuff that has nothing to do with whatever they were arguing about in the first place (it was because of you that I got into trouble in Maths. I covered for you that day, and you never even said thank you). And so it goes on. Before long, they're each convinced that the other is a seriously bad person, and they're using words about each other which I can't print here. After half an hour of this, Ayesha storms off, and she and Alex are no longer talking to each other. They spend that evening on their phones each instructing their group of friends not to talk to their ex-friend who is now their enemy. What a shame. They really liked each other.

Have you ever had an argument like that?

Does it remind you of anything?

It reminds me of a lot of politics today. Someone says (or tweets) something that another group of people doesn't approve of. Instead of trying to understand why they said (or tweeted) it, and explaining why they disagree, they attack the person who said (or tweeted) it, letting them (and the world) know what an awful person they must be. If they can, they get them banned, or fired, or excluded in some way. Of course, this doesn't change the mind of the first person. It just makes her or him (and all the people who agree with what she or he said or tweeted) even more angry about whatever it was they said (or tweeted) in the first place, even more certain that they are right and that anyone who disagrees with them is not just wrong but a bad person. At the end of it, everyone is more intolerant, more angry, more certain of their own

Everyone is more intolerant, more angry, more certain of their own superiority over anyone who disagrees with them

superiority over anyone who disagrees with them, and knows and understands less about whatever it was they disagreed on in the first place. Rather like Alex and Ayesha.

If you shout at the other side, you'll lose

Let's rewind.

Imagine if, instead of shouting at Alex, Ayesha just tells him what she didn't like about what he said or did, and why. Imagine Alex listens to what Ayesha says, carefully. Imagine he then explains why he said or did what she didn't like, and why he thought it was the right thing to say or do. Imagine Ayesha listens to him, carefully, before explaining why she disagrees with him. Imagine Alex listens to her disagreement, before responding, calmly and reasonably, with his own point of view. Maybe Ayesha persuades Alex. Maybe Alex persuades Ayesha. Or maybe they just agree to differ on this one thing, and carry on being friends, carry on liking each other, carry on enjoying each other's company, carry on doing stuff together, carry on respecting each other. Maybe even respecting each other more.

Have you ever had an argument like that?

I hope so. Arguments like that actually bring friends closer.

For three and a half years after the EU referendum, Britain was engaged in the first kind of argument, about Brexit (see Because 6), both sides shouting at each other, both thinking they're right and the other side was stupid, or ignorant, or evil, neither side listening. The United States (at the time I'm writing) is doing much the same about President Trump and his policies. This doesn't make either of those countries a nice place to live; nor does it help anyone to get anything done. It could be better than this. It should be better than this. Shouldn't it?

What has debating got to do with this?

Actually (you won't be surprised to hear) quite a lot.

We'll go more into how debates are judged, how it's decided who won and who lost and why, in Chapter 8, How To Win a Debate. However, I can tell you this now. Debating is a competitive activity - sometimes fiercely competitive - and you should always go into a debate trying to win. But it has rules.

In a debate, if you shout at the other side, you'll lose. If you refuse to listen to them, you'll lose. If you accuse them of being bad people for disagreeing with you, you'll lose. If you call them names, you'll lose. If you make no attempt to understand why they're saying what they're saying, you'll lose. If your speech is the length of a social media post, you'll lose. If your only form of argument is to keep repeating the same thing because you are absolutely certain it is true, you'll lose. And if you are incapable of seeing the world from any point of view other than your own, you'll lose every debate in which you have to argue a case you don't agree with - i.e. about half of them.

On the other hand, if you keep yourself thoroughly informed about what is going in the world, making sure you get your news not only from sources you agree with, you'll win. If you take the trouble to understand both, or all, sides of a question, you'll win. If you listen to those who disagree with you - really listen, until you understand why they're saying what they're saying - you'll win. If you construct your arguments carefully and thoroughly, brick by brick, taking nothing for granted, constantly questioning your own assumptions, you'll win. If you focus on facts and arguments, not people, you'll win. And if you treat the people you debate with respectfully, as opponents, not enemies, you'll win.

If you listen to those who disagree with you, you'll win

What's more, you'll be a much nicer person to be around.

Imagine a world in which everyone - especially people in public life - behaved in the way a successful debater behaves. Wouldn't it be a much nicer, safer, more civilised world? And (just as important) wouldn't it be better run? Wouldn't better decisions get made, if they were only made after the kind of careful, balanced deliberation debating makes you engage in?

One of the reasons I am so passionate about debating, and have devoted so much of my life to promoting it amongst young people, is because I sincerely believe that it can change the world for the better.

It might not seem like it now, but it won't be too long before you and people your age will be in charge. If you can put into practice what you learn from debating in the way you run the world, it will be a much better place.

What have we learnt in this chapter?

1. Debating is something you do anyway, you just need to do it better ☐
2. Debating will make you more sure of yourself ☐
3. Debating will improve your grades ☐
4. Debating is a great way to make friends ☐
5. Debating will help you to understand other people ☐
6. Debating will help you understand the world better ☐
7. Debating will save the world ☐

Now you know why you should do debating, it's time to learn *how.*

That's what we'll do in the rest of the book.

Do this before you read the next chapter

- Persuade a friend to come to debating club with you. Then you'll have used your debating skills to persuade her or him, and you'll have a friend to go to debating club with.

- If you don't have a debating club at your school (yet), find a friendly teacher and persuade her or him to set one up. Then you'll have used your debating skills to persuade her or him, and you'll have a debating club.

CHAPTER 2

How debates work

In this chapter we're going to learn the nuts and bolts of how debates work.

There's more to football than kicking a ball.

There's more to hockey than hitting a ball with a stick.

There's more to playing the clarinet than blowing in one end and moving your fingers up and down.

There's more to debating than just talking.

We need to learn how debates work.

This chapter is going to help do just that.

It will explain the rules of the two main formats of debate in the UK: Mace and British Parliamentary.

What is a debate?

A debate is a structured competition between two opposite points of view.

Who wins the competition?

The side which makes the more persuasive case.

Who decides who made the more persuasive case?

All debates have **judges**. Judges decide who has won the debate. Normally, they use a mark scheme (like teachers do when they mark an exam). Judges also give feedback at the end of the debate telling you what you did well and how you can improve. We will look more at what judges do in Chapter 8, 'How to Win a Debate'.

How do I know what the debate is about?

The topic of the debate is expressed in the motion.

What is the motion?

The motion is a sentence beginning either 'This house would …' (for example, '***This house would make all schools co-educational***') or 'This house believes …', (for example, '***This house believes money does not make you happy.***')

Motions that begin 'This house would …' are about taking action in the world, and are called **policy motions**. Motions that begin 'This house believes …' are about what we think or believe, and are called **ideas motions**.

Whose house are they talking about?

The word 'house' comes from the British parliament. In the British parliament, motions are put forward to be debated by the House of Commons, and at the end of the debate there is a vote to find out what the 'house' (i.e. the House of Commons) either believes or is going to do. As the House of Commons is the law making body in Britain, what the 'house' decides will go on to become to become the law in Britain. (It is useful to know about how the House of Commons works, because how Britain is, or should be, governed is often a topic for debates. We will learn more about this in Chapter 10, What Debaters Need to Know About the World.)

A debate is a structured competition between two opposite points of view

School debating clubs and competitions don't (yet) have that degree of power. In their case the 'house' means everyone in the room listening to the debate, whom you are trying to persuade. In practice, the most important people in the room for a debater are the judges, as they decide who wins.

The most important people in the room for a debater are the judges, as they decide who wins

What actually happens in debates?

- There are two sides: the **proposition**, arguing for the motion, and the **opposition**, arguing against the motion.
- Members of the two sides take turns to speak, with the proposition going first. After that, the debate alternates between opposition and proposition.

Can I speak for as long as I want?

No. There are strict time limits on speeches.

Can I interrupt people on the other side when they are speaking?

Yes. You do this by making **points of information**. There are strict rules about points of information:

- You are only allowed to make points of information during certain times in the speech, known as 'non-protected time'.
- You must stand and say 'on a point of information.'
- If the speaker says 'No thank you', you must sit down without saying anything else.
- If the speaker says 'Yes please', you must make a brief point, no longer than 15 seconds.

Can anyone else speak in a debate?

In some formats, there are **speeches from the floor**. 'The floor' (another term from the British parliament) means the people who are watching the debate.

Now we know the basics of how debates work, we're going to look at the different formats used in competitive debate.

The two debating formats used in the UK are **Mace** and **British Parliamentary**. British Parliamentary is usually known as **BP** for short. There are other formats used in other countries (though many of those countries also use Mace and BP), but for the purposes of this book we will stick with these two, as almost all debating competitions in the UK use one or other of them.

Mace

- The Mace is a large ornamental silver club which rests on a table in the centre of the House of Commons. It is the symbol of royal authority, and if it is not there the House of Commons cannot meet or pass laws. Because debating is what the House of Commons does, the Mace has given its name to a popular format of debating.
- In Mace, there are two speakers on each side.
- They are usually given the motion several days in advance to prepare.
- They speak for seven minutes each, alternating between proposition and opposition.
- The first and last minute in each speech is 'protected' (meaning no one is allowed to make points of information during that time).
- When all four debaters have spoken, speeches from the floor are heard.
- One debater from each side then gives a **summary speech**, lasting four minutes, with the opposition speaking first.
- Marks are awarded for both content of speeches and speaking style.

A variant on the basic Mace format is **Extended Mace**.

- In Extended Mace, there are three speakers on each side.
- The first two speakers on each side speak for seven minutes, alternating between proposition and opposition, with the first and last minute protected.
- Speeches from the floor are then heard.
- Finally, four minute summary speeches are given by the third speaker on each side, with the opposition going first.
- In both formats, the timing of speeches may sometimes be altered if there is less time available / speakers are less experienced.

The two debating formats used in the UK are Mace and British Parliamentary

British Parliamentary

- British Parliamentary (BP) is so called because it is modelled on the way that debates take place in the British parliament.
- There are four debaters on each side, competing in teams of two (so four teams in total).
- Speakers alternate between proposition and opposition.
- Speeches are five minutes each, with the first and last minutes protected. In the middle three minutes, anyone on the opposite side may make points of information.
- There are no speeches from the floor.
- Marks are awarded for content of the speeches only, not for speaking style.
- The speakers are given specific names to reflect the origins of the format in the British Parliament:

  First proposition = Prime Minister

  First opposition = Leader of the Opposition

  Second proposition = Deputy Prime Minister

  Second opposition = Deputy Leader of the Opposition

  Third proposition = Member of the Government

  Third opposition = Member of the Opposition

  Fourth Proposition = Government Whip

  Fourth Opposition = Opposition Whip

  (This incidentally allows you, when you are doing a BP debate, to pretend that you are actually in the House of Commons, debating something that might become law and change the course of history.)
- Titles of motions are not announced until just before the debate. Teams are given only fifteen minutes to prepare, forbidden to talk to anyone but each other, and with no access to any kind of electronic device.

You can pretend that you are actually in the House of Commons

- The teams consist of:

  Prime Minister and Deputy Prime Minister.

  Leader of the Opposition and Deputy Leader of the Opposition.

  Member of the Government and Government Whip.

  Member of the Opposition and Opposition Whip.

- You debate on the same side as people you are competing against. You should not obviously undermine them, but equally you need to look better than them.

- Each speaker has very specific responsibilities, depending on their title / position in the debate. A large part of the judges' verdict will be based on how well you fulfil these responsibilities. We will learn more about this in Chapter 4, Roles and Team Work.

- Judges award each of the speakers 'speaker points'. They add them together to award points to each team. They then put the teams in rank order (first, second, third and fourth) according to how many points they have, and announce this rank order.

- In some BP competitions, there are several debates over the course of a day (usually four, to allow each team to have one go at each position). Teams are ranked at the end of the day first by team points, which are awarded as follows: four for first place, three for second place, two for third place, one for fourth place. If they tie on team points, position is decided by speaker points. The team that comes top of this ranking wins the competition.

Mace is a good format for beginning debaters, because of the longer time you have for preparation, and because it tends to be slightly gentler in style.

BP is more challenging, with more cut and thrust, but also perhaps more exciting.

Each speaker has very specific responsibilities

What have we learnt in this chapter?

1. How debates work ☐
2. The differences between Mace and BP ☐

Do this before you read the next chapter

- Search up some videos of Mace and BP debates online and watch them to see how they work.
- Even better, attend a live Mace or BP competition.

CHAPTER 3

Basic Skills

In this chapter we'll learn the basic skills you need to master to be a successful debater.

Now you know how debating works, it's time to learn the basic skills that every debater needs.

If you want to get good at football, you need to know how to pass, how to tackle, how to take free kicks etc.; if you want to win at tennis, you need to work on your serve, your forehand, your backhand etc. Debating is no different. It can be broken down into certain skills which you can practise and improve.

Here are those skills...

1

Defining the motion

Whoever speaks first in a debate (first proposition) gets to **define the motion**. Your opponents have no choice but to accept your definition, even if they don't like it / don't agree with it. So being given first proposition is a bit like winning the toss in cricket or tennis, or getting white in chess. You get to set the terms; you decide what it is you will be debating about.

How can you make the most of this advantage?

Fencers and boxers stand sideways on, to minimise the area in which their opponents can attack them. In the same way, the best motion definitions will be tight, focused, and precise, to minimise the areas in which your opponents can attack you. A tight and focused definition also allows you to develop your proposition much more fully and thoroughly.

However, before you can define the motion, you first need to analyse it.

You need to understand what kind of motion it is.

Is it a **policy motion**, i.e. one concerned with changing what happens in the world?

Policy motions, remember, begin: 'This house would …'

They call for either:

- something to be done that isn't being done

  or

- something that is being done to be done differently

Two examples of policy motions are:

- This house would give every citizen a universal basic income.
- This house would impose a 20 mph speed limit in all built up areas.

The best motion definitions will be tight, focused, and precise

Policy motions are usually concerned with the *status quo*. This is a Latin term meaning 'the situation at the moment'. They want to either:

A. Introduce a new situation which does not currently exist in the status quo: 'This house would give every citizen a universal basic income' is an example of this. At the time I'm writing, no country in the world has a universal basic income, so this would be an **innovation**, something which does not exist in the status quo.

or

B. Adapt the status quo: 'This house would introduce a 20 mph speed limit in all built up areas' is an example of this. Speed limits already exist, and are part of the status quo; the proposal is to **adapt** the status quo by making them stricter.

Policy motions are about either innovating or adapting

In other words, policy motions are about either **innovating** or **adapting.**

If you're proposing an **innovation**, you need in your definition to answer these questions:

1. **What form would your innovation take?**
2. **How would it be brought into being?**
3. **What would its scope be?**

So, if the motion is 'This house would give every citizen a universal basic income', you need to explain:

1. **How much would the universal basic income be?** (The minimum wage at 40 hours a week? The living wage at 40 hours a week? Current Universal Credit?)
2. **How would it be funded?** (Taxes? National Insurance? Abolishing all benefit payments and replacing them with universal basic income?)
3. **Who would count as a citizen?** (Everyone with citizenship rights over the age of 18? Or over 25? Or over 30? Or people who have already paid a certain amount of tax?)

If you're proposing **adapting** the status quo, you need in your definition to answer these questions:

1. **What will be changed?**
2. **What will be the scope of the change?**
3. **How will this change be implemented?**

So, if the motion is 'This house would reduce speed limits to 20 mph in built up areas', you need to explain:

1. **What counts as a built up area?** (All cities? Where are the boundaries? Residential areas? What do you mean by residential?)
2. **Who will it apply to?** (Cars? Motorbikes? Superfit cyclists? Will emergency services be exempt?)
3. **How will the new law be enforced?** (Speed cameras? Will offenders be fined? How much? Will they have endorsements on their licence?)

In both cases, the more questions (and answers) you (and your debating partner) can think of in the preparation stage, the more precisely defined your motion will be, the easier it will be to propose, and the easier it will be to defend against attack.

The more questions you can think of in the preparation stage, the more precisely defined your motion will be

Alternatively, it might be an **ideas** motion, i.e. one concerned with changing what people think.

Ideas motions, remember, begin with: 'This house believes …'

Two examples of ideas motions are:

- This house believes that money does not bring happiness.
- This house believes that Britain is still a sexist society.

For **motions of ideas**, you do not need to explain what action you would take.

Instead, you need to define how you understand the meaning of the words.

So, for 'This house believes that money does not bring happiness', you need to explain:

- **What do you mean by 'happiness'?** (Emotional well-being? A sense of purpose? Feeling loved? Having a good relationship with God?)
- **What do you mean by 'money'?** (Everyone needs some money to survive - do you mean having more than this does not bring happiness? Do you mean having too much gets in the way of happiness? How much is too much?)

Be specific and precise

In the case of 'This house believes that Britain is still a sexist society', you need to explain:

- **What do you mean by 'society'?** (Formal institutions such as the media? The justice system? Education? The world of work? Or the way that people interact with each other in everyday life?)
- **What do you mean by 'sexist'?** (Discrimination with a practical impact, e.g. unequal pay, women being denied promotion etc.? Attitudes expressed in speech, writing and the media which demean women? Or institutional structures, e.g. laws about parental leave?)

Again, the more questions (and answers) you (and your debating partner) can think of in the preparation stage, the more precisely defined your motion will be, the easier it will be to propose, and the easier it will be to defend against attack.

So, when you're defining:

- **Be specific and precise**
- **Pay attention to detail; anticipate problems**
- **Be clear about what you think words mean**

And one last thing ... once you've defined your motion, make sure you and your partner stick consistently to that definition all through the debate.

2 The mechanism

When you debate a policy motion (one that begins 'This house would …') you are trying to persuade your listeners to take action in the real world.

The 'would' implies a 'how'. How exactly would you do what your motion is proposing you should do? This is what is known as the **mechanism**. It only applies to policy motions.

The mechanism is owned by the proposition, specifically the first speaker for the proposition. It is an important part of defining the motion (see above).

Let's take an example: the motion 'This house would tax meat'. This is an excellent example of a policy motion which needs a strong mechanism, because it is very broad and general. So, if you're proposing it, how do you go about constructing the mechanism?

It's a good idea to start by defining the long term goal which is implicit in the motion. Here it is twofold: a healthier environment (fewer farting cows) and healthier diets (more vegetable based meals). The greater the impact the mechanism has, the closer you'll get to the goals.

How exactly would you do what your motion is proposing you should do?

All right then, let's propose a 1,000% tax on the sale of all meat products. That will turn everyone vegetarian overnight, apart from a few super rich people. Cows get made redundant, no one has heart disease any more. Big impact. Job done.

The 1,000% tax would certainly produce a massive impact. Unfortunately, it would also incur considerable costs:

- Massive unemployment in industries related to producing and distributing meat.
- Massive resentment, alienating all but the most fanatical from your well-intentioned policy.
- Massive evasion of the tax, and quite possibly a criminal black market in meat.

So, go too far with your impacts and you can end up creating much bigger costs which outweigh the beneficial impacts, leaving you open to attack from the opposition. A historical example of excessive costs is Prohibition. From 1920 to 1933 the sale of alcohol was prohibited in the United States. It was described as the 'Noble Experiment', with the intention of preventing the damage drinking did. Instead, the law was widely disrespected, and organised crime gangs became enormously powerful.

All right then, let's minimise the costs. We'll just go for a 1% tax on streaky bacon. When it's sold in packs of four. On Thursdays. That's a tax, and it's on meat.

That will annoy no one. It is almost impossible to criticise. It will also have virtually no impact on the environment or on dietary choices, so will get you nowhere near the long term goal implied by the motion.

So what's the answer?

The art of constructing an effective mechanism is to find the sweet spot somewhere between the impacts and the costs, maximising the former, minimising the latter. In this case, a 10% tax on all sales of meat would be about right; enough to nudge people towards different behaviour while still being enforceable.

Find the sweet spot between the impacts and the costs

But there's more to constructing an effective mechanism.

As well as hitting this balance between **impact** and **costs**, the mechanism also needs to be:

- **Practical** - something that can be done.
- **Enforceable** - something that people will accept.
- **Simple** - something that can be explained in less than five minutes.

The 10% example meets these criteria. There is plenty of precedent for taxing the sale of certain products, e.g. cigarettes, showing it can be done, so it is **practical** and **enforceable**; and it is **simple** enough to be explained and grasped in the short time allowed in a debate.

What do you do with the mechanism if you are the opposition?

You have to accept the mechanism as constructed by the proposition, in the same way as you have to accept the motion as defined by the proposition. Look for its weaknesses: if it has too many costs (the 1,000% tax example), attack the costs. If it has too little impact (the streaky bacon example) attack the lack of impact. If, on the other hand, the proposition have managed to hit the sweet spot, you're probably best off leaving it alone, and focusing instead on the principles implicit in this motion, in this case defending people's freedom to buy and eat what they like.

So, to sum up:

If you're the proposition:

- Find the sweet spot between impact and cost.
- Keep the mechanism practical, enforceable and simple.

If you're the opposition:

- Find the weakness in the mechanism and attack it.
- If it's a strong mechanism, leave it alone and go for principles instead.

Keep the mechanism practical, enforceable and simple

3 Signposting your speech

I love walking in the countryside.

However, sometimes it is quite a stressful experience.

When I walk in the English countryside, much of my time is taken up with looking at the map, holding it sideways, upside down, the wrong way round, looking at this tree and that mountain, trying to work out if we should have turned left at that stile or right at that stream, trying not to argue with whomever I'm walking with. This is partly because I'm rubbish at map reading, but it is also because there are very few signposts in the English countryside.

When I walk in Switzerland, though, it's a different matter. There, they have neat, tidy, yellow signposts every mile or so pointing you in the right direction and telling you that it is 1 hour and 10 minutes to the lake, 1 hour and 40 minutes to the river, and 2 hours and 5 minutes to the town (where you will find toilets, a bus stop and a cafe serving hot chocolate, with vegan options also available). Walking in Switzerland (doing most things in Switzerland) is a very low stress experience.

What has this got to do with debating?

You want your listeners to have a low stress experience as they listen to your speech. Make your speech like Switzerland. Fill it with signposts, telling the listeners where you are going.

Make your speech like Switzerland

- Say what you're going to say.
- Say it.
- Say you've said it.
- Then say it again.
- Don't be afraid of repetition.
- Above all, don't be afraid of repetition.
- Repetition is not something you should be afraid of.

To expand:

- Start by stating what your three points are (and don't have more than three).
- Then introduce your first point.
- Amplify and expand on your first point.
- Remind everyone what your first point was.
- Repeat this for each of your three points.
- Finally, remind everyone what your three points were.

Say what you're going to say. Say it. Say you've said it. Then say it again. Don't be afraid of repetition.

See what I just did? You won't forget my point about signposting. If you use signposting well, your listeners won't forget your points either.

And remember: amongst your listeners are the judges, who decide who wins the debate. Signpost well, and they will remember your argument. You need to remember something before you can understand it. You need to understand something before you can be persuaded by it. Debates are won by the side who are more persuasive. So effective signposting can point you the way to victory.

4 Speech paragraphs

Paragraphs are, along with sentences, the building blocks of writing. They give it structure and shape. Although debate speeches are a spoken, not a written, form of expression, they too need paragraphs to give them structure and shape.

The most common structure for a speech paragraph is **PEEL**. This may be familiar to you already, as it is similar to the paragraph structures often taught to students in English and History lessons.

PEEL stands for:

Point: What you're trying to say, in one sentence.

Explanation: Amplfying what you want to say

Evidence / Example: Something concrete to back up what you want to say

Link: Connecting what you've said back to the motion.

So, for example, given the motion 'This house would make all schools co-educational':

Point: 'Co-educational schools help children to learn how to get on with the opposite sex.'

Explanation: 'If children spend all their time at school with their own gender, they will never understand the opposite sex. This will seriously disadvantage them in later life, when they will have to live and work with people of the opposite sex.'

Evidence / Example: 'A woman who has been educated entirely in girls' schools will find it very hard to assert herself if she ends up working in a male-dominated profession. Had she had years of having to do this in class, she would be much better prepared.'

Link: 'School should be preparing children for life, and single-sex schools obviously do not do this. This is why they should not be allowed to exist.'

PEEL is a very helpful format for constructing your speech. As you become a more experienced and confident speaker you may be able to dispense with it and be more flexible in your style (this is also true of paragraph structures in writing). But when you are starting out, it is worth hanging on to.

Debate speeches need paragraphs to give them structure and shape

5 Points of information

The first time you watch a debate, you will see something strange.

Every few seconds, someone will stand up and interrupt whoever is speaking. This seems very rude. Sometimes the person speaking will tell the interrupter to sit down. This seems rude too.

It isn't rude. Points of information are a vital, vital part of debating. So vital, in fact, that you can't win a debate without them.

'Points of information' is a rather confusing, perhaps outdated term (but we're stuck with it for now). Points of information do not have to convey any information. They do, however, have a point. Let's look at:

- How to make them as a listener.
- How to receive them as a speaker
- How to make them work for you as a listener.
- How to make them work for you as a speaker.

Once in that middle period it is time to pounce

How to make points of information

Speakers have what is called 'protected' time, usually a minute, at the beginning and end of their speech. Trying to make points of information during that time is against the rules, and is also discourteous and makes it look like you are not paying attention, so is not a good idea. The timekeeper or chair will indicate when protected time begins and ends with an established signal, usually a knock on the table.

Once in that middle period, though, it is time to pounce. You make a point of information by standing up and saying 'On a point of information'. That's all; you don't say anything else yet. If the speaker says 'No thank you', you have to sit down. If the speaker says 'Yes please', you then make your point. It must be brief – maximum 15 seconds. So it has to be concise and, yes, to the point. When you've made your point, you must sit down. You're not allowed to say anything more until your next point of information. It isn't a conversation.

Make at least one point of information a minute, even though they won't all be taken. Don't, however, make them one after another. This is called 'badgering' (see below), is considered discourteous, and may be penalised by judges.

If you make no points of information, you will almost certainly lose the debate.

How to receive points of information

If you are speaking and someone stands up and says 'on a point of information', you don't have to stop in mid sentence. Finish your point first, then say either 'Yes please' or 'No thank you'. Don't leave them standing too long before you do this. Remain calm and courteous. Let them have their say, and don't respond till they have sat down.

Take at least one but not more than two points of information.

If you take no points of information, you will almost certainly lose the debate.

How to make a point of information work for you as a listener

Debating is as much about finding the flaws in the other side's arguments as it is about promoting your own. Points of information are your opportunity to expose the flaws in the other side's argument while they're in the middle of making it. Think of them as being like a shot at goal in football. That shows how important they are: in football, you might have beautiful passing, but you'll never win a match if you don't score any goals; in debating, you might have beautiful arguments, but you'll never win if you don't make points of information. So you need to be listening to the speech, hard. You need to be thinking hard too. You need to be on the lookout for a crack in their argument, and you need to jump in and prise open that crack as soon as you see it.

You'll never win if you don't make points of information

There are essentially two types of points of information:

- **Practical:** finding the practical flaws in a proposed course of action.

  Like this example, in a debate on 'This house would make the use of homophobic language a criminal offence.'

  Speaker for the proposition: 'Homophobic language on social media causes great distress to gay people, and this law would protect them from it.'

  Opposition: 'On a point of information'

  Speaker for the proposition: 'Yes please.'

  Opposition: 'How will you deal with homophobes who post on anonymous, untraceable accounts?'

- **Fundamental:** finding the contradictions in the logic of an argument.

  In the same debate, on the other side:

  Speaker for the opposition: 'Criminalising homophobic language will allow homophobes to present themselves as martyrs for free speech.'

  Proposition: 'On a point of information.'

  Speaker for the opposition: 'Yes please.'

  Proposition: 'If an action causes harm to society, it should be criminalised, and we should not be deterred from fighting crime by the reaction of the criminals and those who would justify their actions.'

Make your points of information fast, hard and on target

Notice also how a point of information can be presented either as a question (preferably a really hard one) or a statement (preferably a really convincing one). Notice, too, that one sentence is enough. The shorter the better. Save the elaboration of argument for your own speech. Back to football: a shot at goal is more likely to go in if it is fast, hard and on target. Make your points of information like that.

How to make a point of information work for you as a speaker

You must, of course, rebut the point. Simply ignoring it and carrying on with your speech is (still on football) like stepping back and letting the other side kick the ball into your goal. It should instead be like the goalkeeper catching the ball and immediately kicking it upfield to the striker, who will take it deep into the other side's half.

Respond quickly, crisply, and decisively. They tried to find flaws in your argument; find flaws in their point of information. Then go back to your argument. Even better - a really advanced skill - weave your rebuttal of their point of information into your own argument.

Let's see how that might work in practice.

Speaker for the proposition: 'Homophobic language on social media causes great distress to gay people, and this law would protect them from it.'

Opposition: 'On a point of information'

Speaker for the proposition: 'Yes please.'

Opposition: 'How will you deal with homophobes who post on anonymous, untraceable accounts?'

Speaker for the proposition: 'They may be untraceable for now, but once this proposition becomes law, the whole apparatus of law enforcement will be used to find technological means to trace them, catch them and prosecute them. The prospect of this happening will be enough to deter these hateful people whom the other side would protect on the grounds that it might be too much trouble to find a solution to a technical problem.'

See? You're taking the ball into their half by making it look as if their actions will protect homophobes.

Or …

Speaker for the opposition: 'Criminalising homophobic language will allow homophobes to present themselves as martyrs for free speech.'

Proposition: 'On a point of information.'

Speaker for the opposition: 'Yes please.'

Proposition: 'If an action causes harm to society, it should be criminalised; we should not be deterred by the reaction of the criminals and those who would justify their actions.'

Speaker for the opposition: 'Much greater harm would be caused to society by the surge in popular support for homophobic bullies which this unnecessary law would bring about. A tolerant culture which allows everyone to express both their sexuality and their opinions is a far more effective sanction against prejudice than a heavy handed and unnecessary law.'

See? You're taking the ball into their half by making your defence of free speech work also as a defence of gay rights.

So, to sum up:

If you're listening:

- Make at least one point of information a minute
- Make them short and sharp
- Aim them at a weak point in the argument

If you're speaking:

- Take at least two points of information
- Rebut them fully but concisely
- Make your rebuttal lead back into your speech

Take the ball into their half

6 Rebuttal

The 1992 comedy *My Cousin Vinny* is not perhaps the greatest movie ever made. It does, however, have one memorable scene. The main character, Vinny, is a lawyer, hired to represent his cousin, who has been falsely accused of involvement in an armed robbery. Vinnie isn't, it's fair to say, at the top of his profession; he's failed his law exams six times. However, he is cheap. So cheap that the only hotel he can afford is next to a railway line that keeps him awake all night. As a result, he falls asleep during the prosecution's opening submission. Prompted by the judge to respond on behalf of his client, Vinny stirs himself, strides confidently towards the bench, and says, 'Everything that guy just said is garbage.' (Actually, he doesn't say, 'garbage'. He says something else. You can search up the clip online to find out what he really says.) Vinny's response is a very good example of how not to do rebuttal. Unfortunately, the Vinny technique is still all too common, both in debating and in life.

The better your reason, the better your rebuttal

So, how can we do rebuttal better than poor old Vinny?

Let's look at:

- **What rebuttal is.**
- **Why you should do rebuttal.**
- **When you should do rebuttal.**
- **How you should do rebuttal.**

What is rebuttal?

Rebuttal is when you challenge, criticise or find fault with your opponent's argument **with reason.** I'll say that again: **with reason**. It is different from simply saying someone is wrong. This is the Vinny approach, which itself is the mirror image of the argument known as 'simple assertion'. (We'll learn more about that argument and what's wrong with it in Chapter 7, Thirteen Bad Arguments.) No reason, no rebuttal; but the better your reason or reasons, the better your rebuttal.

Why do rebuttal?

Without rebuttal, a debate becomes a series of performances: one free standing speech after another, none of them having any connection with each other. No matter how well composed the speeches are, they might as well have been written down, photocopied and handed out to the audience. In fact, you might as well not even be in the same room. A debate without rebuttal is like someone who behaves as if there is no one else there. Have you ever met anyone like that? They're not much fun to be with. With rebuttal, however, a debate becomes a conversation; a conversation where people actually listen to each other. It becomes dynamic, unpredictable, unsafe. In other words, it comes to life. A debate with rebuttal is a lot harder, but it's also a lot more interesting and, ultimately, more fun.

When should you do rebuttal?

A. At the beginning of your speech

Unless you are first proposition, you are always speaking just after someone on the other side has spoken. You need to show you have actually listened to that speech by responding to what has been said, and by saying, **with reason**, why you disagree with it.

B. In points of information

Despite their name, points of information are essentially forms of rebuttal. They are your chance to engage with the other side's argument in a targeted way and to find fault with it.

C. When discussing the point of clash

Once you've identified the point of clash, you then have to show you have won the debate by rebutting the other side of the clash. What is 'the point of clash'? We'll find out later in this chapter.

With rebuttal, a debate comes to life

How do you do rebuttal?

Rebuttal is the work of analysing an argument and finding its weaknesses. It's really hard work, and it doesn't get any easier. You just have to keep practising it. The more you practise it, the better you will get at it. This will have benefits not just in debating, but in life, as you are less likely to be fooled by people who look as they're talking sense but aren't really.

There is a whole section of philosophy, called 'critical thinking', dedicated to analysing arguments and their strengths and weaknesses. You may have studied it at school. For now, though, here are some very simple tools for understanding how arguments work.

Arguments consist of **premises** and **conclusions**. In a strong argument, the premises lead to the conclusion. So, for example:

- Anna is a person (Premise 1)
- All people are mortal (Premise 2)
- Therefore, Anna is mortal (Conclusion)

Or, to put it more like a mathematical formula:

- A is B
- All Bs are C
- Therefore, A is C.

There are three main ways to challenge an argument:

1. **One or more of the premises is weak.**
2. **The premises do not lead to the conclusion.**
3. **The premises are strong and do lead to the conclusion, but the conclusion is undesirable.**

Let's see how these would work in practice.

Take the motion: 'This house would make all schools co-educational.'

Someone puts this argument:

'All schools should be forced to be mixed, because when girls and boys attend the same school, they have to spend time with each other, so they learn to get on with the opposite sex, which is a vital life skill.'

Let's analyse that argument.

Premise 1: Mixed schools make boys and girls spend time together.

Premise 2: Spending time with people teaches you to get on with them.

Premise 3: Getting on with people is a vital life skill.

Conclusion: Therefore, all schools should be mixed.

Arguments consist of premises and conclusions

How can we rebut?

Now let's see how we could rebut it.

Challenging Premise 1

'Mixed schools don't make boys and girls spend time together. They spend most of their time ignoring each other. At break time the boys play football, the girls talk. Students at single-sex schools spend much more meaningful time with the opposite sex, because when they do so, they do so out of choice.'

Challenging Premise 2

'Putting boys and girls together doesn't make them get on with each other. Boys tend to dominate class discussion, intimidating girls into not giving their opinions. This establishes a very unhealthy dynamic for later life, where men make decisions and women listen; not a good way to "get on with each other". Girls in single-sex schools get the confidence to express their opinions in class much more easily, and are thus better equipped to interact with men on an equal basis in later life.'

Challenging Premise 3

'Girls consistently achieve better exam results in single-sex schools. Making them sacrifice this achievement by forcing them into mixed schools so they can "learn how to get on with boys" is sending out the message that socialisation is more important than success; or, to put it another way, it's more important for a girl to be nice than to be clever. Is that how we should be bringing up our daughters?'

Showing that the premises do not lead to the conclusion

'It may be true that boys and girls spending time together at school can teach them how to get on better in later life, but that doesn't mean all schools should be forced to be mixed. Not all children are the same; some thrive in single-sex environments, and shouldn't be forced into a "one size fits all" model.'

Questioning the desirability of the conclusion

'Shouldn't schools be about academic education, not socialisation?'

Or:

'What business does the government have telling us what sort of education we should choose for our children?'

So, as you can see, there are many different ways you can rebut even a simple argument like the one above. We'll be learning more lines of attack in Chapter 7, Thirteen Bad Arguments, in which we'll learn how to spot flawed arguments and how to challenge them. But with five possible lines of attack just for that one simple argument we chose (often there will be more), you have to choose. You can't say all those things at once.

How do you choose? Challenge your opponent where her argument is weakest. Look through the rebuttals above, and decide for yourself which exposes the most weakness in the original argument.

To sum up:

- Rebuttal is essential for debate
- Do it at the beginning of your speech; in points of information; and when summing up.
- Simple denial is never enough.
- Break your opponent's argument down to premises and conclusion, and challenge it at its weakest point.

By the way, all the rebuttal arguments above can of course themselves be rebutted. Debating is not about finding a final definitive truth, nor is it an activity suited to people who need there to be one and only one answer to every question. This might be why North Korea have never done very well in the World Schools Debating Competition. In this respect debating teaches us something very profound, and something that would make the world a much better place if more people understood it. As the nineteenth century English writer John Henry Newman wisely advised:

'Never stop searching for the truth; never trust anyone who tells you they have found it.'

Challenge your opponent where her argument is weakest

7 The point of clash

Debating is a competitive activity. Two teams clash against each other, and one comes out the winner. But it isn't only the teams that are clashing. It's also the ideas. That's where 'the point of clash' comes from.

The 'point of clash' is the hinge of a debate

What is the 'point of clash'?

The 'point of clash' is the essence of the debate. It is where the fundamental disagreement between the two sides lies. All the other disagreements simply derive from that first disagreement.

You could think of it as the hinge of a debate. As with the hinge of a door or a window, it is the part that all the other parts are attached to. It is also the part that stays still to allow the other parts to move.

Let's go back to 'This house would make all schools co-educational', and see how the point of clash applies to that motion.

We saw in the last section on rebuttal that an argument often made for the motion is that co-educational schools teach children how to relate to the opposite gender better. This, it is argued, benefits girls as much as boys, because they will have to work with men for the rest of their lives, so they might as well get used to what they're like early on.

An argument often made against the motion is that girls perform better academically in girls' schools. To give an example, in a girls' school they are more likely to choose science subjects in the sixth form, as it will not be perceived as a 'boys' subject', and they are more likely to have women science teachers as role models.

Suppose the debaters choose to focus on those two arguments. Let's look at the principles behind them.

The argument for the motion assumes that **social** education is more important; that the best way to get on in life is to get on with other people. The argument against the motion assumes that the **academic** side of education is more important; that the best way to get on in life is to get good grades. So there you have the clash: **social vs academic**.

If you're debating this motion, you need to keep coming back to that point of clash, **social vs academic**, ensuring that everything you say builds up your side of the clash and exposes the flaws on the other side.

A common mistake is to get distracted from the point of clash by marginal issues, often practical ones, e.g. how much more complicated it is for parents who have a son and daughter at single sex schools to have to interact with two different schools, or how students in mixed schools are constantly being distracted from their lessons by attractive boys / girls. (Students at mixed schools tend to find that this is rarely an issue first lesson on a wet Wednesday in November when half the class got up too late to have a shower.)

A successful debater, though, will focus all her arguments behind either the social or the academic benefits, ensuring that her arguments for the greater importance of the social / academic are stronger, and that the weaknesses in the arguments for the greater importance of the other side are exposed. She will also make sure that, in her summary, she reminds the judges what the point of clash is, and shows them how she has won the clash, saying: 'They said this … we said that … we won because…'.

Bear in mind, too, that the same motion may generate different points of clash in different debates. To take the co-educational schools example, the two sides might instead disagree over whether the government has the right to tell people what sort of schools their children should go to. Those for the motion would say that the benefit to society of co-education is more important; those against it would say that the right of parents to make their own choices for their children is more important. The point of clash would then become quite different: **collective benefit vs individual freedom**. Usually what the point of clash is will become clear when the motion is defined by the first speaker, who should be setting the terms of the debate, if they do what we advised above when defining the motion.

Show how your side has won the clash

So, to make the point of clash work for you:

- If you are the proposition, identify the point of clash clearly in your definition of the motion.
- If you are the opposition, analyse the proposition's definition in order to identify where the point of clash will fall in this debate.
- Keep ruthlessly focused on it; don't waste time on marginal issues.
- Refer to it in your summary, and show how your side has won the clash.

8 Stakeholder impact analysis

We said in the section above on the **mechanism** that policy debates are about making things happen in the real world. Those things happen to people.

The people are called **stakeholders**.

Debates are about making things happen in the real world

What happens to them is called impact.

Understanding the impact that the action proposed by the motion will have on various groups of people will help you to define and defend your case more effectively if you are the proposition, and to attack it more successfully if you are the opposition.

This process is called **stakeholder impact analysis**.

How does stakeholder impact analysis work?

Let's go back to 'This house would make all schools co-educational.' The first question to consider is: whose lives would be changed if this motion was enacted? In other words, who are the stakeholders?

Here's a list:

- School students
- Parents
- Teachers
- Employers
- The government

The next task is to work out what impact the proposed change would have on each of these groups. In other words, what **impact** would the change have?

A good approach is to draw up a table like this:

STAKEHOLDERS	IMPACT
School students	They would all have to attend co-educational schools.
Parents	They would no longer have the choice of sending their children to single-sex schools.
Teachers	Those who had only worked in single-sex schools (or preferred working in single-sex schools) would have to learn the different skills required for teaching both boys and girls.
The government	Changing single-sex schools to mixed schools would take up a great deal of the Department for Education's time and money.
Employers	Eventually, everyone in the country would have attended a co-educational school. Would this make them better or worse at their jobs?

Now, once you've decided stakeholders and impact, place the stakeholders in rank order as to how important you consider their interests to be. There isn't a right answer to this exercise, but how your ranking comes out reveals how you will approach the debate.

Place the stakeholders in rank order

Suppose you choose this rank order:

1. **Students**
2. **Parents**
3. **Government**
4. **Teachers**
5. **Employers**

The assumption this ranking reveals is that schools are there to meet the needs of the children who attend them. If you are the proposition, this will lead you to argue for the benefits co-education will bring to school students, e.g. the greater ease they will feel with the opposite sex. If you are the opposition, it will lead you to argue for the costs it will bring to school students, e.g. worse grades for girls. The point of clash will then be **social benefits vs academic benefits**, but it will be focused around how those benefits impact students personally.

What, though, if you came up with this order?

1. **Employers**
2. **The government**
3. **Teachers**
4. **Parents**
5. **School students**

This would imply a very different approach to education. This suggests a world in which children's needs are seen as less important than the needs of society as a whole. The purpose of education in this order of priorities is to fit children for the world of work. So, the proposition might argue that co-educational schools prepare children better for the world of work because they teach them to collaborate better with the opposite sex as they will have to in the workplace; the opposition might argue that single-sex schools are more likely to produce women engineers and scientists, and that this is what the economy needs. The point of clash will still be **social benefits vs academic benefits**, but those benefits will be entirely from the point of view of employers, and to a lesser extent the government. The question the debate will have to answer is: which type of schools will bring more benefit to the national economy?

Or suppose another rank order:

1. **Parents**
2. **Teachers**
3. **School students**
4. **Employers**
5. **The government**

This ranking implies a **libertarian** approach. Libertarianism means maximising people's freedom of choice. If parents are the most important people when it comes to their children's education, they should be allowed to choose how their children are educated; it is not the government's business to tell them what to do. Similarly, teachers should be able to choose what sort of school they want to work in, and students should be able to choose what sort of school they attend. If employers or the government don't like those choices, bad luck. This approach only really works for the proposition for this motion. The point of clash will be **individual freedom vs. collective benefit**. If you are the opposition facing this kind of proposition, you have to try to move, in your arguments, the rank order so that employers and government go further up, thus tilting the debate away from freedom and back towards collective benefit.

To sum up:

When preparing for a debate:

- Work out who will be affected by the proposed change.
- Work out what impact it will have on them.
- Decide which group of people you think is most important.
- Frame your argument accordingly.

Work out who will be affected by the proposed change

9

How to prepare

There are two kinds of preparation: long preparation, where you are given several days to prepare a motion, popularly known as **long prep**, and short preparation, popularly known as **short prep**, where you are given a much shorter time, usually 15 minutes, to prepare.

Mace uses long prep; BP uses short prep.

Let's start with short prep.

Every minute - every second - counts

Short prep

It can feel like a pretty scary prospect, having to speak in front of a room full of people, half of whom will be disagreeing with every word you say, about something you knew nothing about until 15 minutes ago. Even more so when your phone and / or tablet has been surgically removed from you (as is the rule in all debating competitions), and you have nothing to rely on but your naked brains and those of your debating partner.

Every minute - every second - counts in that prep time. So, how to make the best use of those precious quarter of an hour?

Get to the room as fast as you can (this could easily use up two minutes, depending on how big the building you are competing in is and how good your sense of direction is).

Make sure you have:

- Paper
- Several pens or pencils
- Highlighters
- Index cards
- A bottle of water

Now you're in the room, alone with each other. What to do first?

You should both keep quiet for five minutes.

Why? Surely we should be discussing, sharing our ideas? Well, yes, but you have to have some ideas to share first. It's quite possible you will never have thought about the motion topic in your life. Even if the topic is one on which you have both deep knowledge and passionate convictions, you need some time to gather your thoughts. And if you gather your thoughts separately, you'll have twice as many thoughts by the end of the prep time. So, for five minutes silence should fall again, as you scratch away with your pens.

What are you writing about?

You need to be asking yourself questions; big questions.

There are **seven** big questions which apply to any policy motion, and which you should always ask.

1. **What is the debate about?**
2. **What do we have to prove?**
3. **What do they have to prove?**
4. **What will be changed if the motion is passed?**
5. **Who are the actors?**
6. **Who are the stakeholders, and what impact will the motion have on them?**
7. **What is the mechanism?**

Write or type these questions out on a piece of card and bring them to every debate.

If the motion is an **ideas motion**, the questions will be fewer, which in some ways is easier, and in other ways is harder. For an ideas motion you need to ask:

1. **What is the debate about?**
2. **What do the words in the motion mean?**
3. **What do we have to prove?**
4. **What do they have to prove?**

How might you answer these big questions in practice?

Let's take some examples. First, preparing the policy motion 'This house would tax meat', with you proposing. As we said earlier, it's a nice big, broad motion (only four words long) with lots of scope for interpretation.

You need to be asking yourself questions

1. **What is the debate about?**

   This question is asking you to cut through all the practicalities and focus on the essential point of principle. Here, the debate is about whether the state has the right to intervene in the market for the benefit of society as a whole. It's about which is more important: the individual or the collective.

2. **What do we have to prove?**

   You are proposing a change to the status quo. First you have to prove there is a problem with the status quo; then you have to prove that your proposed change will solve the problem. There will always be both costs and benefits associated with any change, and you have to prove that the benefits of your proposed change will outweigh the benefits. So, you have to prove that: consumption of meat has bad consequences; taxing it is an effective way to lessen those consequences; the benefits of taxing meat will be greater than the costs.

3. **What do they have to prove?**

   As they're defending the status quo, they have to prove either that the status quo works and does not need changing, or that it does need changing but that your way of changing it will either not work or that its costs will be greater than its benefits. (They may also choose to propose a better way of dealing with the problem presented by the motion.) So, they have to prove either that the consumption of meat is not a bad thing (or is even a good thing), or that it is a bad thing but that taxing meat is not the way to deal with it, either because it will not work, or because the costs will be greater than the benefits.

4. **What will be changed if the motion is passed?**

   Most debate motions say, 'The world will be a better place if we take this action.' So, what will the world look like if your proposed action happens? It's worth considering both short and long (and sometimes medium) term impacts. In the short term, everyone will eat less meat, and the government will have more money. In the long term, climate change will be greatly slowed down now that thousands of acres of land are filled with health giving plants rather than farting cows, and everyone will be slimmer and healthier thanks to their vegetable rich diet; those few who persist in eating meat will be treated for the diseases brought on by their diet in shining new hospitals paid for by the tax on their addiction.

What will the world look like if your proposed action happens?

5. **Who are the actors?**

   This means who is going to make the change happen. Here, it is the government, as they are the ones who are going to be setting and collecting the tax.

6. **Who are the stakeholders and what will be the impact on them?**

   This means, as we learned above, the people who are affected by the change. Here, it is the government, livestock farmers, retailers, consumers and the population in general. The impacts are that the government will have more tax income; livestock farmers and retailers will lose income; consumers will have to pay more for meat; and the population in general will benefit from the environmental and health benefits of a tax on meat. How you rank the importance of these stakeholders will determine how you approach the debate.

7. **What is the mechanism?**

   The mechanism is about how will you make the change happen. Here, you get into the nitty gritty. How much tax? 5% of the price? 10%? 25%? Will you add it to the price in shops, or to the price retailers pay to farmers? Which is most likely to achieve the benefits you seek while minimising the costs? Having a high tax rate would be more likely to put people off buying meat; having a low tax rate would make it easier to get popular support for the measure, and would make black market evasion of the tax less likely. As we learnt in the section above about the mechanism, you need to find the sweet spot that maximises impact and minimises costs.

Now let's look at how to propose an ideas motion: 'This house believes that money does not bring happiness.'

1. **What is the debate about?**

The key word is 'happiness'. Once you know what that is, it is much easier to make your arguments. As the proposition, you need to focus on non-material aspects of happiness, things that can not be bought, such as love, friendship and emotional well-being.

2. **What do the words in the motion mean?**

'Happiness' we have already dealt with. 'Money' looks quite easy to

Who is going to make the change happen?

define. However, the motion doesn't tell us how much money. You are probably best off defining it as a more or less infinite amount, so that you can argue that the trouble with money is that you no matter how much you have you could always have more, so you are always dissatisfied, so you are never happy.

3. What do we have to prove?

That certain things bring happiness, and that none of them depend on money; or alternatively, that depending on money to make you happy will never be successful, because you can always have more money, and therefore will be permanently dissatisfied and unhappy.

4. What do they have to prove?

The opposition have to prove that the things that bring happiness depend on money and cannot be achieved without them. They are likely therefore to focus on things that money can buy, such as material security, good healthcare and the opportunity to support your children.

You need to have answers to these questions jotted down in the first two minutes. Yes, two minutes. You have to think fast as a debater.

Next, you need to take up another sheet of paper and start brainstorming arguments for both sides (still without talking to your debating partner). Do this for three minutes. In this three minutes, you need to switch off the part of your brain that keeps telling you that what you're doing isn't very good. Don't worry whether the arguments are good or not; just get them down, as many of them as possible. Quantity is more important than quality at this stage. Selection comes later.

You have to think fast as a debater

The five minutes are up. You look up from your notepads. Your eyes meet.

What do you do now?

First, you share your answers to the big questions, and make sure you agree on the answers. Once you've done that, it will be easy to agree how you're going to define the motion (see defining the motion on page 35 on how to do that). With the big answers and the motion definition clear in your minds, you can proceed to the arguments. Go through the ones for your side of the motion first.

Choose the six most persuasive. Then rank them according to their persuasiveness. The first speaker gets the top three in order of persuasiveness, the second speaker gets the next three in order of persuasiveness. Note, no more than three arguments each. Time to reach for the index cards now. Take one for each of your three arguments. On it, write a headline, which should be no more than a word or at most a phrase, and short points on how you're going to expand on it.

With the motions we've picked, a card for the 'meat' motion might look like this:

HEALTH

- *Excessive consumption of meat = major cause of heart disease and diabetes.*
- *Taxing it discourages consumption, nudges consumers towards healthier choices by making them cheaper.*
- *Heavy taxation on tobacco = massive reduction in smoking = major health benefits; taxing meat = same.*

Time to reach for the index cards

A card for the 'money' motion might look like this:

LOVE

- *Being loved = happiness.*
- *Love that is paid for is not love.*
- *Money can corrupt relationships, e.g. being friends with / marrying someone for their money.*
- *True love does not depend on money. e.g. marriage vow 'for richer, for poorer'.*

The smallness of index cards has two advantages:

1. It makes them easier to handle while you are speaking, ensuring you spend more time making eye contact and less time fumbling with your notes.
2. It ensures your notes are concise and focused.

Boiling your speech down to three index cards will also help you to signpost it better (see above on how to signpost on page 41).

I'll just take a moment here to say something very important.

NEVER, NEVER, NEVER write out a debate speech in full.

That isn't debating; it's essay writing.

You can be good at writing essays and good at debating, and you can learn a lot about how to write essays from doing debating, but they are NOT THE SAME THING.

NEVER, NEVER, NEVER write out a debate speech in full.

I hope I made that clear.

This sorting out of your own arguments should take another five minutes. Now it's time to consider the other side's possible arguments and how to rebut them. Do this by taking turns, one person stating the arguments, the other one rebutting them. As well as working out what you will say in rebuttal, this will both get you into the mind set of the other side (which is vital), while also sharpening up your rebuttal responses. It's a bit like footballers passing a ball around to warm up just before kick off.

The point of clash should be your guiding star

Your final task is to find the point of clash (see the advice above on the point of clash on page 53). This should be the thing you keep in mind all the way through the debate, your guiding star. You need to keep coming back to it, and keep showing the judge that you are on the winning side of it, particularly if you are speaking last. Very often, it will be the answer to the first question: what is the debate about? Here, the point of clash in the policy motion is the right of the state to intervene to protect the health of the community against the individual's right to make their own choices. You have to show that the damage that meat eating causes to health and the climate outweighs the loss of freedom entailed by a tax on meat. In the ideas motion, the point of clash is whether happiness is brought by material or non-material things. You have to show that while material things are important, they are neither as durable nor as reliable sources of happiness as non-material things. Say the point of clash to each other a few times, as a kind of mantra, to make sure it is at the front of your mind.

By now, your brain should be singing, and you should be ready to talk for England (literally, if you are representing England in the World Schools Debating Competition). If you're feeling nervous, embrace it. As every actor, performer and sportsperson knows, that adrenaline rush will sharpen up your performance and make you more focused. Gather up your notes, take a swig of water, and head for the debating chamber.

Long prep

Essentially, do everything as above, only do it more slowly. Set aside an evening (or lunchtime) by yourself for the initial silent preparation; then get together with your debate partner for another evening (or lunchtime) to share ideas and plan.

One significant difference between long prep and short prep is of course that with long prep you are allowed to research the topic, in particular to use the internet. This is both a blessing and a curse. It can help you to feel more confident if you have more facts and examples at your fingertips; however, there is a danger that you can be so weighed down with facts and examples that you lose sight of the arguments. Remember, debates are won by the quality of arguments. Facts and examples are only there to support the arguments. So, while it might be helpful to accumulate a lot of data in the first phase of your preparation, once you start refining your arguments, you should be ruthlessly selective and only use data that supports your central argument.

That adrenaline rush will sharpen up your performance

Also, be careful (especially on the internet) with the sources of your research. Not all websites are equally reliable. In general, websites that are associated with established institutions like universities, the BBC, the NHS, or the UK government are more likely to be accurate than those run / contributed to by people who have no obvious expertise or experience in the topic. Books, newspapers, magazines and journals are even more reliable than the internet, as they have editors who check facts. It helps, too, to consider plausibility: is a website that argues that 9/11 was organised by the US government in order to collect the insurance money, or that the grieving relatives of victims of school shootings are in fact just actors paid by people who favour gun control, likely to be reliable?

Books are more reliable than the internet

10 How to deal with debaters behaving badly: squirrels and badgers

One of my most vivid memories of childhood is of my father - normally the most gentle and peaceable of men - going red in the face, shouting and banging on the window. This wasn't because my Mum had chucked him out and changed the locks. It was because, again, a squirrel was raiding the bird feeder in the back garden.

Squirrels can be pesky beasts in the back garden. They can also be pesky beasts in debating, when someone 'squirrels' the motion.

What is 'squirrelling'?

Squirrelling happens when the motion is defined in a way that is either absurdly narrow, or goes quite against the obvious sense of it.

So, if the motion is 'This house would ban cars from Central London', a squirreller might choose to define 'Central London' simply as Oxford Street (the main shopping street). If the motion is 'This house believes Britain is a racist society', a squirreller might choose to define 'a racist society' as one where neither the head of state nor the head of government is black. In the first case, they set up a mechanism which has so little impact that it can barely be criticised (hardly anyone would notice if cars were banned from Oxford Street). In the second, they set the bar for the counter-measure from the opposition impossibly high: a large number of people would have to die before we got a black monarch; getting a black Prime Minister is more plausible, but is not likely to happen before the end of the debate (unless it has happened by the time you read this book ...).

Squirrelling is, like stealing the bird feed from the birds, a sneaky, rather petty thing to do. It gives the proposition an unfair advantage. It is not strictly against the rules of debating, but it is not well regarded either. It gives the impression that you're not good enough to win the debate on fair and equal terms. I would not let my teams do it as a coach, and it would not impress me as a judge.

What should you do if you face squirrelling?

You have to accept the proposition's definition of the motion, no matter how absurd; that's one of the fundamental principles of debating (see above on defining the motion on page 35). So, tackle the definition full on, on its own terms. If they call for banning cars from Oxford Street, talk about the congestion this would cause in the surrounding area. If they say not having a black Queen makes Britain racist, talk about how many leading politicians are from ethnic minorities. The judge will respect you for having the courage not to flinch from the challenge presented by the distinctly uncourageous act of squirrelling.

On to our second pesky animal. Quite why the peaceable, hard working **badger** has been associated with the habit of aggressive questioning, I don't know. Still, to 'badger' someone is part of the English language, and also of the language of debating. Badgering happens when one side makes points of information over and over again and / or in an aggressive tone. Some particularly ruthless teams will seek out whoever they perceive to be the weakest speaker on the other side and deliberately target them for badgering. Like squirrelling, it isn't strictly against the rules, but, like squirrelling, it doesn't go down well with judges and it certainly isn't something I would let my debaters do. Points of information work best on a 'quality, not quantity' basis.

What should you do if you're badgered?

Don't let them get to you. Keep going with your speech. Don't forget you are in control and they can only speak when you let them. Accept one or two points of information, but no more. The judge will respect you for keeping calm under pressure.

Don't forget you are in control

Good debaters don't need to squirrel or badger. The quality of their arguments speaks for itself. Make yourself that sort of debater.

11

How to speak

I've left this to last, even though some people think it is the most important. It isn't. Quality of arguments is what will win a debate. That said, how you speak is important. In Mace, it is part of the mark scheme; in BP it isn't, but a judge can't help favouring a speech that is delivered in a way that is engaging and easy to listen to.

How you speak is important

Here are some basic principles for how you should deliver your speeches:

1. **Speak loudly enough.** Speeches that can't be heard are not likely to be persuasive.
2. **Speak clearly.** Mumbled, unclear speeches are also not very persuasive. However, provided you are clear, you needn't be afraid of speaking fast. Normally, when advising people about giving readings or speeches in public, I advise speaking slowly, to allow the audience to take in what you are saying. Debating is different, however; you have a lot of content to get in, and you need to make the most of every second of your limited time.
3. **But don't shout.** No one likes being shouted at. Aim to speak to the furthest away person in the room. If you have difficulty with projecting your voice, ask for help from a drama teacher.
4. **Make eye contact.** It makes the people who are listening feel like you are talking to them. If you never look up from your notes, they will feel like you don't care about them. Choose a different person to make eye contact with for each section of your speech. Don't forget the judges. However, don't make continuous eye contact with only one person throughout your speech. They might think you are either threatening them or trying to pick them up.
5. **Vary your tone and your pace.** Talking in the same way throughout your speech is boring.
6. **Use emotion.** Sound like you care about what you are arguing for, or against.
7. **Use timing.** A slowing down of pace, or a dramatic pause, just before a major point will give it more impact.
8. **Study the great speeches of history.** Analyse how they use language to persuade. I particularly recommend Abraham Lincoln's Gettysburg address; Martin Luther King's 'I have a dream' speech; Barack Obama's speech on the night he was first elected President in 2008; and Mark Antony's 'Friends, Romans, countrymen' speech in Shakespeare's *Julius Caesar*. You can find either the originals or performances of all these speeches online.

What have we learnt in this chapter?

1. How to define the motion ☐
2. How to use the mechanism ☐
3. How to signpost your speech ☐
4. How to construct speech paragraphs ☐
5. How to use points of information ☐
6. How to do rebuttal ☐
7. How to use the point of clash ☐
8. How to do stakeholder benefit analysis ☐
9. How to prepare ☐
10. How to deal with squirrels and badgers ☐
11. How to speak effectively ☐

Do this before you read the next chapter

- Watch some debates online (or live), each time focusing on how the debaters use just one particular skill, e.g. rebuttal, signposting, points of information etc. Make notes on how they use this skill well, and what they could have done better.

- If you are in a debating club, watch a debate online together, dividing up the skills you are going to comment on between you. Then have a discussion, chaired by your teacher, in which you compare notes.

- Alternatively, have some members of the club conduct a debate and others observe them, each taking responsibility for commenting on a particular skill. Take turns doing this, so everyone gets to debate at some point. Even better, film the debate and then watch it and analyse it together.

CHAPTER 4

Team work and speaker roles

In this chapter, we're going to learn about how to work as a team, and about the different roles different speakers have.

Debating is a team activity. To be a good debater, you need to be a good team worker. The teams are small - two, or at most three - and this makes team working skills even more important; you depend on each other.

Debating also involves taking on roles, and in this respect is a little like acting. As in acting, you need to enter into the personality of someone who is not you. This can be both liberating and exciting. You take on a role when you speak for a motion you passionately disagree with, or against a motion you passionately agree with. You also take on a role when you speak, as different speakers have different roles to play depending on where they speak in the debate.

Let's start with team work.

It's often said that 'There is no I in team' (conveniently forgetting that there is a 'me'). Team work is about putting the interests of the team above your own. Your objective as a team member is not to make people listen with awe, admiration or even laughter to your speech; it is to win the debate. So here are some basic principles for team work as a debater, which will help you to win debates together:

- Analyse honestly your own strengths and weaknesses as a debater, and discuss them with your partner(s). Think about how your strengths can balance her / his / their weaknesses and vice versa.
- When preparing together, make sure you all have more or less equal air time. Don't be too dominating in discussion; but don't be too quiet either.
- Divide up the points for your speeches between you clearly and stick to that division. Make sure not to repeat your partner's points or, worse, contradict them.
- When your partner is speaking, look interested: nod approvingly, make a serious face at the serious points, shake your head when she condemns something, laugh when she makes a joke. This will be encouraging for her, and may also subliminally influence the judge.
- Have a stack of index cards on the table in front of you during a debate. If, while your partner is speaking, she needs a key fact, or you can see a useful point she could make, write her a note on a card and pass it to her. (Speaking to your partner while she is speaking is not allowed, but passing notes is.)
- Always congratulate your partner after a speech, however it has gone. Use back slaps / high fives / hugs as appropriate. Analysis of what went wrong can wait till later.

Your objective as a team member is to win the debate

Now let's look at roles.

Make it brief, but clear

First proposition (in BP, the Prime Minister)

The first thing you have to do as first proposition is define the motion. Look again at the section on defining the motion in Chapter 3, The Basic Skills, page 35. This should take about 10% of your speech.

Once that's done, you have to set out not just your own argument, but your whole side's arguments. In BP, this will be you and the Deputy Prime Minister; in Mace, you and your second speaker.

Make it brief, but clear. 'I will be arguing that A / B / C. The Deputy Prime Minister / my partner will be arguing that C / D / E.' (Remember, three points only per speech.) This signposting helps the audience (crucially, the judges) to follow your case easily. Spend about 20% of your speech on this.

Then, get going with your speech, covering your three points, devoting the other 70% of your time to it. One advantage of speaking first is that you do not have to do any rebuttal. Make the most of this advantage by making your arguments as thorough as possible.

First opposition (in BP, Leader of the Opposition)

Your first task is rebuttal of the first proposition speech. Look again at the section on rebuttal in Chapter 3, The Basic Skills, page 48. Spend about 20% of your speech on this. Then set out your case and that of your partner / the Deputy Leader of the Opposition in the same way as above for the first proposition; another 20%. Then 60% on your own arguments. Remember, you must accept the definition offered by the first proposition, so you may need to think fast and adapt your arguments if it is different from what you expected / prepared for.

Second proposition / opposition (in BP, Deputy Prime Minister / Deputy Leader of the Opposition)

Rebuttal of previous speaker, 20%; then your own arguments, 80%.

Government Member / Opposition Member (BP only)

This is in some ways one of the most challenging positions. Because you are in a team of two with the Government Whip / Opposition Whip, you are competing not just against the other side but also against the first two speakers on your side. You must not, however, contradict them (this is known as 'kniving'); however, neither should you waste any time supporting their arguments. Instead, support their definition of the motion, but do it better than they have.

You do this by **extension**. That is, you must find **new** arguments and **new** examples supporting the motion as it has been defined by first proposition. This calls for some quick thinking, as you don't know what the first two speakers on your side are going to say until they say it.

You still have to do rebuttal of the previous speech; still 20%.

Third proposition (in BP; Government Whip / Opposition Whip)

The key thing to remember in this role is that **you must not introduce any new material**. The reason for this rule is that it is unfair to the other side, as they have no opportunity to rebut it.

You do not need to rebut the previous speaker in the way that all the other speakers except for First Proposition have. Instead, your job is to **sum up the debate**. Summarise the cases made by both your side and the opposition, showing where you clash (see the section on the point of clash in Chapter 3, The Basic Skills), and showing why your side has won that clash. 'The proposition have argued that … however, we say that … / we have argued that … the opposition claim that … however, this is not the case because ….' Spend slightly longer on your side of the case and, of course, make it sound better. You must refer to the first and second speakers on your side, and make their arguments sound good (remember, in BP, even though you are competing against them, you still need to make them sound good; it will earn you points from the judges.)

What makes a good summary?

What makes a good summary? Think of yourself as a teacher, explaining your case, with the judges as your students. Most teachers do what they call 'plenary' at the end of a lesson or a unit of work, in which they sum up what has been covered in a way that makes it as clear and memorable as possible, so that their students understand it and remember it. If the judges understand and remember your case, they are more likely to be persuaded by it, and to award you the debate. Think of how your best teacher does plenary, and try to emulate her or him.

To be successful in this role, you have to be an excellent listener and a quick thinker. You must be able to take in everything that is said in the debate and organise it in a clear, logical way under pressure of time. Efficient note taking skills are useful here (also very useful in your school studies!). You also have to be good at identifying the points of clash and focusing rigorously on them in your summary.

Keep focused on the main point of the debate

Summary speaker (Mace) / Third speaker (Extended Mace)

Everything said above about Government / Opposition Whip applies, with the addition that you must respond to / rebut speeches from the floor.

One other responsibility of all speakers, and a key aspect you will be marked on, is making points of information (see the section on points of information in Chapter 3, 'The Basic Skills'). You should aim (subject to not being guilty of 'badgering') to make one or two points of information to every speaker. Even if they are not accepted, the judges will see that you are trying, and will reward you accordingly. Equally, if you do not make any, they will penalise you for this.

Whatever your role, keep rigorously focused on the main point of the debate; don't allow yourself to be sidetracked into marginal issues. If the debate is about making it compulsory for 50% of MPs to be female, and you find you are spending 50% of your time discussing the cost of removing urinals from toilets in the Houses of Parliament, you are not really focused on the main point, which is about whether using quotas is the best way to tackle discrimination.

Working as a team, and fulfilling the role you have been given, are both key parts of any debating mark scheme. This is right, because both are essential parts of making the most persuasive case possible

What have we learnt in this chapter?

How to be:

- First prop ☐
- First opp ☐
- Second prop ☐
- Second opp ☐
- Third prop ☐
- Third opp ☐
- Summary speaker ☐
- A good team worker in debating ☐

Do this before you read the next chapter

Watch a debate online, or stage one in your debating club, and make notes analysing how well each speaker has fulfilled their role.

CHAPTER 5

How to get from Now to Then

In this chapter we'll be learning about how to build an effective proposition case.

Debating is about changing the world.

Actually, it isn't, most of the time, unless it's a debate in parliament which results in a law being passed. However, policy motions - which are the most commonly used motions - are about changing the way things are. Understanding this will help you, if you are the proposition, to build an effective case.

A helpful way to think of building the case for change is to think in terms of **NOW**, **THEN** and **ACTION.**

NOW is the situation as it is.

THEN is where you want to get to.

ACTION is what gets you from **NOW** to **THEN**

The **ACTION** is what is at the centre of the motion; it's what comes after 'This house would …'

The ACTION is the centre of the motion

In order to make a case for the proposition, you need to prove that:

1. **NOW** is not good.
2. **THEN** would be better.
3. The **ACTION** will get us to **THEN.**

You need to answer the following questions:

1. What's the **NOW**?
2. What's wrong with **NOW**?
3. What will **THEN** look like?
4. Why will **THEN** be better?
5. How will the **ACTION** get us to **THEN**?

So, how would you do this in practice?

Let's take a very concrete policy motion: 'This house would make it compulsory for all 18 year olds to do a year of community service.'

1. What's the **NOW**?
   - 18 year olds can do what they want when they leave school; go to university, get further training, get a job, or do nothing all day.

2. What's wrong with **NOW**?
    - Young people think only of their own future, without any sense of the needs of others less fortunate than themselves.
    - As a result, society is very fragmented and lacking in solidarity.
    - Young people only learn a narrow set of skills.
    - Young people have little experience of the lives of people who are not like them.
    - Many young people, who do not have places at university / jobs with prospects, lack a sense of direction and purpose.
    - Charities and voluntary organisations helping less fortunate people are understaffed.
3. What will **THEN** look like?
    - Every 18 year old would spend a year, before beginning study or work, helping people less fortunate than themselves.
4. Why will **THEN** be better?
    - Society will be more open minded, as people would grow up with a broader experience of life.
    - Society will be more united, as people would have a shared experience at a formative age.
    - Society will be more compassionate, as people would have been confronted with people less fortunate than themselves.
    - All 19 year olds will be equipped with basic, transferrable skills.
    - Charitable / voluntary projects will never be understaffed.
5. How will the **ACTION** get us to **THEN**?
    - By making the year of community service universal, with very few exceptions, this law would ensure all the benefits listed above.

Think in terms of NOW, THEN and ACTION

Thinking in terms of **NOW**, **THEN** and **ACTION** is a very helpful way to break down, and then build up, a proposition case. It is also, by the way, a very useful skill to have in life, whenever you want to persuade people to embrace a change you think is desirable, whether that's being loaned money to launch a new business; radically changing our way of life to cut carbon emissions; or being allowed to move into your sister's bedroom now she's gone to university.

However, any case is of course open to attack. That's what the opposition is for (and what you need to do if you're the opposition.)

And that's what we'll look at in the next chapter.

What have we learnt in this chapter?

How to break down a proposition case into:

- **NOW** .... ☐
- **THEN** .... ☐
- **ACTION** .... ☐

Do this before you read the next chapter

Analyse, either by yourself, by discussing in your debate club with your debate coach, these motions, in terms of NOW, THEN and ACTION.

1. This house would ban parents from driving their children to school.
2. This house would decriminalise drugs.
3. This house would abolish GCSEs.

Thirteen reasons why... you're wrong!

In this chapter, we're going to be learning about lines of attack for the opposition.

We've seen how to make a case for change. However, not all change is good. Sometimes change needs to be stopped. If you're the opposition in a policy debate, your job is to persuade people to reject the proposed change.

Sometimes change needs to be stopped

Here are thirteen ways you can do this;

thirteen lines of attack.

1. The problem addressed by the motion doesn't exist. (There's nothing wrong with **NOW**.)
2. The definition of the problem is wrong. (**NOW** is bad, but not for the reasons you say.)
3. The action proposed by the motion won't lead to a solution of the problem. (**ACTION** won't get us to **THEN**.)
4. The action is impractical. (**ACTION** won't work.)
5. Even if the action works, it is inherently wrong in itself (**ACTION** is immoral / undesirable.)
6. The action will only cause more problems in the long run (**ACTION** will make a **THEN** that is worse than **NOW**.)
7. The solution proposed is inherently wrong in itself. (**THEN** is immoral / undesirable.)
8. There's a different, more important problem. (There's a worse **NOW** somewhere else.)
9. The solution won't be any better than what we have now. (**THEN** will be no better than **NOW**.)
10. There is a better solution to the problem. (Our **ACTION** will get from **NOW** to **THEN** better than yours.)
11. There is no solution to the problem. (You're never going to get to **THEN**.)
12. The solution has already been tried and has failed. (The **ACTION** didn't get from **NOW** to **THEN** in the past, so it won't now.)
13. The problem will go away without the solution you propose. (We'll get from **NOW** to **THEN** without **ACTION**.)

Let's see how you might use these **lines of attack** with the motion we discussed in the last chapter: 'This house would make it compulsory for all 18 year olds to do a year of community service.'

1 The problem addressed by the motion doesn't exist.

Young people already have a great many useful skills, which they have learnt at school and elsewhere, and will continue to learn in further study. Many of them already work with people less fortunate than themselves; most schools have some sort of charity outreach, and the very popular Duke of Edinburgh scheme has a compulsory community service unit. 93% of young people attend non-selective state schools which introduce them to a whole range of people unlike themselves. So compulsory community service would be addressing a problem which doesn't exist.

2 The definition of the problem is wrong.

Young people are not lacking in skills and social solidarity because they don't do community service; it's because schools are too focused on competitive public exams, which teach a narrow set of skills and pit schools and individuals against each other to move up league tables / get university places. The exam system is the source of the problem you have identified.

Young people already have a great many useful skills

3 The action proposed by the motion won't lead to a solution of the problem.

It's a good idea for young people to learn new skills and work with people less fortunate than themselves, but most of the community service is likely to be low skill activities like picking up litter or cleaning toilets, which will not teach them anything new or introduce them to the people they are supposed to be helping.

4 The action is impractical.

There are about half a million young people in any given age cohort in the UK. Funding them all to do community service would be vastly expensive; organising them would require paying many more people. What would be done with young people who refused to take part / didn't turn up? Chasing them up / sanctioning them would also be time-consuming and expensive. There simply aren't enough community service projects in existence to keep all these people busy; we'd have to create unnecessary work for them. Moreover, more privileged / well connected families would find ways to get their children out of having to do the community service, undermining the purpose of introducing more privileged young people to those less fortunate than themselves.

Community service is a kind of slavery

5 Even if the action works, it is inherently wrong in itself.

While community service is a good thing, it is a serious infringement of human rights to force people into it unwillingly. The government telling people what to do for a whole year of their lives is tyrannical, the sort of thing that only happens in dictatorships. It is a kind of slavery.

6 The action will only cause more problems in the long run.

Making community service compulsory would cause so much resentment amongst young people that they would never want to do any voluntary or charitable work ever again; charities and voluntary organisations would suffer as a result. That resentment would mean that the work done as part of the community service would be done much worse than that done currently by genuine volunteers, and charities and voluntary organisations would suffer from that as well.

7 The solution proposed is inherently wrong in itself.

A society where everyone has to do the same thing between the ages of 18 and 19 is not one we want to live in. It will create a uniformity of thinking and a regimented atmosphere that would be oppressive. Compulsory shared activities, however admirable in themselves, are the hallmark of dictatorships, not democracies.

8 There's a different, more important problem.

There is a problem with divisions in society between those who are less fortunate and more fortunate, and also in the lack of purpose, direction and skills that many young people have. However, this is caused by the unfair economic system, which ensures that children of rich parents go to socially exclusive schools and get the best jobs, while children of poorer families do not have the same opportunities. This economic injustice is what needs to be addressed; forcing young people unwillingly into community service is just avoiding the real problem.

Forcing young people into community service is avoiding the real problem

9 The solution won't be any better than what we have now.

How is a year resentfully picking up litter and cleaning toilets going to turn everyone into more compassionate, caring, highly skilled and purposeful citizens?

10 There is a better solution to the problem.

A year of community service at age 18 is an excellent thing for young people to do and would bring all the benefits you describe. However, we propose a better way to promote it; instead of making it compulsory, make it voluntary but incentivised. Anyone who did a year of community service before going to university would automatically have their tuition fees paid by the government. Given that young people who go to university tend to be predominantly from more privileged backgrounds, this would be an excellent way to introduce them to people less fortunate than themselves. Also, because it would be a free choice, the resentment that compulsory community service would breed would not be an issue.

11 There is no solution to the problem.

Of course it would be lovely to live in a world where everyone was forced to be caring, compassionate and altruistic, and there were no divisions between people of different backgrounds. People tried to build a world like that in Russia in the twentieth century, and look what happened: economic ruin and millions of people starved, shot and imprisoned. Human nature is not like that, and never will be.

12 The solution has already been tried and has failed.

From 1949 to 1960, all 18 year old men in Britain had to do two years of compulsory military service. It is now widely acknowledged that this was not a success. Training the conscripts, many of whom were not fitted for the military life, put the armed forces under unnecessary strain, while the compulsory nature of the service bred resentment, hatred of authority and, in many cases, criminality in impressionable young men. There was also compulsory military service in the United States during the Vietnam War in the 1960s, but it was often evaded by young men from privileged families, with the result that most of the soldiers came from less privileged backgrounds, in which African-Americans were over represented, worsening rather than healing social divisions. There is no reason to suppose that compulsory community service would not face very similar problems.

13 The problem will go away without the solution you propose.

With the development of artificial intelligence taking over many jobs, people will have more leisure time than ever before. They will want to spend this time in meaningful, worthwhile activity, and as a result charities and voluntary organisations will have volunteers flooding through their doors, with all the benefits that this will bring both for those organisations and for the volunteers themselves.

You can see already that some of these arguments are stronger than others. Different motions will lend themselves to different lines of attack, and part of the job of the opposition is selecting the best lines of attack. Also, on a practical note, there simply won't be time in one speech (or two speeches across a team) to use all thirteen lines of attack. However, it is helpful to have them written down somewhere (for example, by bringing this book to debates) to refer to in preparation time. Think of them as a toolkit; you need to select the best tools from it for the job in hand. You can, of course, use some or all of these tools when persuading someone in real life not to do something you do not want them to do, or not to make you do something you do not want to do (see how useful debating is for life?).

The job of the opposition is selecting the best lines of attack

What have we learnt in this chapter?

- Thirteen different lines of attack .... ☐

Do this before you read the next chapter

Go through all the arguments against compulsory community service in this chapter, putting them in rank order, with 1 being the best, 13 the worst. Compare your ranking with the other members of your debating club and discuss with them and your debating coach why you have placed them in this order. What makes a strong argument? What makes a weak argument?

Apply the lines of attack above to the three motions we looked at at the end of the last chapter. How would you use them with that motion? Discuss with other members of your debating club which lines of attack will work best with which motion and why.

The motions were:

1. This house would ban parents from driving their children to school.
2. This house would decriminalise drugs.
3. This house would abolish GCSEs.

CHAPTER 7

Big fat fallacies

In this chapter we're going to be looking at bad arguments: what's wrong with them; how not to use them; how to attack your opponents if they use them.

Debating is about making arguments, but it is also, equally and just as importantly, about critiquing arguments.

'Critiquing' something is not the same as to criticising it; it means analysing it, seeing what works and what doesn't. You need to learn how to critique your opponents' arguments, but you also need to learn how to critique your own arguments, testing them out, finding what are the strong points and what are the weak points.

A very helpful way of critiquing arguments is to be able to detect logical fallacies. A logical fallacy is an argument that looks as if it makes sense, but in fact does not. Once you know about logical fallacies, you start detecting them everywhere. Then you can make sure you don't use them yourself, and attack your opponents when they do.

In this chapter, we're going to be learning:

- What some of the most common logical fallacies are.
- What's wrong with them.
- How to respond if your opponent uses them.

You must have a reason for everything you say

1 Simple assertion

There are some situations in life - choosing your lunch, deciding what to wear to a party, getting married - when it is better not to go into all the reasons. Doing so can waste a lot of time, and even end up pushing you into the wrong decision.

Debating, however, is not one of those situations.

You must have a reason for everything you say. Always. ***Always, always, always***.

This is where our first logical fallacy comes in: **unsupported assertion**.

What is 'unsupported assertion'?

It's when you say something is true without saying why it is true.

Supposing you say in a debate, 'Obviously co-educational schools are a better preparation for life,' and leave it at that. You don't explain how or why. You don't consider the arguments against them being a good preparation for life. You don't show why those arguments are less strong than yours.

What you just did was **unsupported assertion**. You have not proved that what you said is true. And proving that what you say is true is what debating is all about. Assertion is only the starting point; everything depends on the proof. Unsupported assertion is like writing the title of an essay, but not writing the essay; it's like putting all the ingredients for a meal on the kitchen counter, but not cooking the meal; it's like putting the ball on the penalty spot but not kicking it. You get the picture. It's starting the job but not finishing it.

What should you do if your opponent does it?

It's a very easy argument to rebut, partly because it isn't really an argument at all. If you're on the side of single-sex schools and your opponent says, 'Co-educational schools are obviously a better preparation for life' and nothing more, you have only to say, 'She has told us that co-educational schools are a better preparation for life, but she has not shown us how or why.' This will remind the judge that your opponent has been guilty of unsupported assertion, and she will be marked down accordingly.

To sum up:

Unsupported assertion is when you say something is true without saying why. Don't do it. Don't let your opponents get away with it.

2 Playing the player, not the ball

Imagine two young children arguing about football in the playground.

> ***'Chelsea are better than Man United.'***
>
> ***'Man United are better than Chelsea.'***
>
> ***'Chelsea are better than Man United.'***
>
> ***'Man United are better than Chelsea.'***

Play the ball, not the player

So far, they're using our first logical fallacy: **unsupported assertion**.

Let's see what happens now.

> ***'You only support Man United because you're stupid.'***
>
> ***'People who support Chelsea are a load of stuck-up Londoners.'***

They've now moved on to a new logical fallacy. It has a Latin name: the *ad hominem* - literally, to the person. Or, to put it another way, and to use a metaphor appropriate to the preceding discussion, playing the player, not the ball.

The *ad hominem* is used when you attack the person making the argument ('you'), or a person or people associated with the argument ('stuck-up Londoners'), instead of the argument itself (which team is better, Man United or Chelsea). In football, if you play the player not the ball, you give away a free kick; in debating, if you attack the person not the argument, you give away speaker points.

Obvious, you might say. I don't do that. I don't go into debates calling the people on the other side stupid / ugly / boring / saying they've got no friends, or even saying they're talking rubbish because they come from a rubbish school. But there are more subtle forms of the *ad hominem* that are still flawed, but are all too commonly used. Let's look at some examples, and how to rebut them.

You cannot say to anyone 'you cannot make that argument'

The 'check your privilege' argument

A. 'The proposal that 50% of places on science courses at university should be reserved for women is wrong because it would be unjust to exclude men who have better grades than women simply because of their gender.'

B. 'Point of information. As a man, you can have no understanding of the difficulties women face in making a career in science, the unjust discrimination they have suffered for so many years, and you have no right to talk about injustice.'

It may be true that women have suffered discrimination in science-related employment for many years; it may be true that they still do. This could be a strong argument for the need to introduce quotas to address this injustice. The fact, however, that the person making the argument against quotas is a man has nothing to do with the argument. You cannot say to anyone 'you cannot make that argument'; you can only say, 'that argument is a bad argument because …'

So how should A rebut this?

There's a bad way:

A. 'Women who say that just want to get an unfair advantage when it comes to university applications.'

This is the equivalent of kicking back at someone who has kicked you. It will end up with both of you being sent off.

And there's a good way:

A. 'I don't dispute the injustice that women have suffered, and still do suffer, from discrimination. It is real and it is wrong and it should be tackled. However, introducing a different kind of injustice through the use of quotas is not the way to deal with this problem.'

Here, like a footballer stepping out of the way of the flying boot and regaining possession of the ball, A moves away from the personal attack and gets straight back on to the main point of the argument.

Move the debate back on to the argument

The 'they don't get it' argument

A. 'Parliament should vote for the UK to rejoin the EU because Brexit is a disaster for the British economy.'

B. 'Point of information. MPs are overwhelmingly white, male and privately educated. How can they possibly know what is best for ordinary people?'

This looks less like the *ad hominem* because B is not attacking the speaker. She is, however, attacking people associated with the argument, not the argument itself.

Bad rebuttal:

A. 'It's a good job they're privately educated. It means they've got more sense than all those idiots who voted for Brexit.'

Kicking back, attacking a different group of people.

Good rebuttal:

A. 'That is a very fair point about the unrepresentative nature of Parliament. However, this debate is not about how MPs are selected. It is about Britain rejoining the EU. And the reason Parliament should vote for the UK to rejoin the EU is …'

Gently but firmly moving the debate back on to the argument.

The 'you can't tell me that' argument

A. 'Making the use of homophobic language illegal would be counter-productive because it would turn bigots into martyrs.'

B. 'Point of information. As a gay person, I have suffered homophobic bullying. You have no right to tell me that the law should not protect me from this.'

This is a harder one to deal with, partly because it often comes with a very emotional personal story. It can feel like any form of rebuttal is a personal attack. That shouldn't blind you to the fact that it is itself a personal attack. It is saying to the first speaker, because you haven't experienced what I've experienced, you are worth less than me.

Here's how to rebut it without letting things get personal:

A. 'I'm very sorry to hear that you've suffered that kind of bullying. It is totally wrong and indefensible. I want to see an end to that kind of bullying. That's why I'm against the proposed measure, which will only make homophobic bullying worse because ...'

Again, gently but firmly leading us back to the argument.

To sum up:

- Don't attack the person making the argument.
- Don't attack people associated with the argument.
- Always attack the argument.
- If the other side do 1 or 2, don't attack back, but instead lead the debate gently but firmly back to the argument.

In other words ... ***keep your eye on the ball***.

3 Argument by anecdote

'One death is a tragedy; a million deaths is a statistic.' So said Joseph Stalin. Stalin is perhaps not the ideal role model for a debater, given that, during his brutal reign as leader of the Soviet Union, he had millions of people murdered for daring to question a single word he said. However, he did have a point.

Individual stories - also known as **anecdotes** - are always more emotionally powerful than generalised statistics. As such, they can be very persuasive. If a charity wants to raise money to help girls in less economically developed countries attend school, a story about little Aisha who wants to be a doctor when she grows up because she saw her mother die of malaria and ever since she's wanted to make other women better is always going to have people reaching for their credit cards faster than graphs and charts extrapolating levels of female education as correlated to mortality rates. So it's not surprising that debaters often reach for these stories in the hope of persuading audiences and judges.

Individual stories are always more powerful than statistics

The trouble is that an **argument by anecdote** is not a valid argument. Why? Because it can only provide proofs about one person, or at best a small group of people. You can't make a general proof from a sample of one, or very few.

You can't make a general proof from a sample of one

Let's take an example. In a debate on the motion, 'This house would make all schools co-educational', a speaker against the motion tells us a moving story about her best friend, Harriet. Harriet started out at a co-educational school, but was miserable there because the boys all mucked about in English, her favourite subject, so she couldn't learn anything. Her parents took her out and put her in a girls' school, where everyone wanted to work, and now she is getting top grades in English. This proves that girls' schools always get better results.

Does it? What does this anecdote actually prove? It might prove that the English teacher in Harriet's first school wasn't very good at keeping order. It might prove that the English teacher in her second school was better at keeping order and also better at teaching English. It might perhaps prove that, for Harriet, a girls' school is the better choice. What it doesn't prove is that girls' schools always get better results.

How could the speaker have made the argument better?

She could have looked up data about exam results, which does, in fact, show that girls' schools tend to get better exam results than co-educational schools. That's girls' schools from across the country - so a large sample, therefore stronger evidence. If it was a short prep debate, where she wouldn't have access to this research, she could have made a more general point about the way in which girls tend, in general, to be more conscientious and eager to please their teachers, and are therefore more likely to achieve good exam results (why this might be and whether or not it is a good thing are both matters for discussion and, perhaps, debate). Of course, neither of these arguments would have the personal, emotional appeal of Harriet's story. But they would be much stronger arguments, and much more likely to win the debate.

What should you do if someone uses argument by anecdote against you?

It can be hard rebutting **argument by anecdote**, because it can feel like a personal attack, especially if the anecdote is particularly emotional or revealing. In this respect it is a bit like the 'check your privilege' argument we covered under the 'Playing the Player, not the Ball' logical fallacy. It is possible, however, both to respect the anecdote and to rebut the argument, by first pointing out that, while the anecdote may be true, it only applies to one person and one situation, and by then broadening the argument back out to general questions.

So, if you found yourself faced with Harriet's story, you could say 'I'm sorry that your friend had a bad time at her first school, and I'm glad that she's happy at her new school. Maybe that first school just wasn't right for her; maybe there were other reasons that she was unhappy, that had nothing to do with it being co-educational; maybe it just wasn't a very well run school. Well run co-educational schools are the best option for all children because ...' and off you go, back to the wider arguments for your side of the case.

It's hard giving up anecdote, precisely because it is so appealing. It's also used very widely to persuade, both in advertising and in politics. But **argument by anecdote** is not honest argument; it will be marked down by judges, and it will lose you the debate.

To sum up:

- Evidence must come from a wide base.
- One person's story is not enough to prove anything.

4 Argument by democratic majority

Democracy. Rule of the people, by the people, for the people.

We all love democracy. We all believe in it. It's a good thing, isn't it? What's more, it's compulsory. It's one of the British Values which all schools are obliged by law to teach. Democracy is like God used to be four hundred years ago; we can argue forever about what it means, but no one is allowed not to believe in it.

Debating helps democracy to work better

Democracy is a good thing, and debating is at the heart of it. Debating helps democracy to work better, because it provides a safe, respectful, balanced way for people to manage their differences, and this is what democracy should be doing.

However, while democracy is a good way to run a country, it is not a good way to prove anything. This leads us to our fourth logical fallacy: **argument by democratic majority**.

I hear it all the time in debates. '57% of people think we should legalise marijuana ...77% of people want to keep the monarchy ... a survey was done and most people thought this was a bad idea.' One issue with these kinds of statements is the unreliability of opinion polls: their complete failure to foresee the results of the UK General Elections in 2015 and 2017, and the Brexit referendum and the US presidential election in 2016, does not inspire confidence. However, even if they were 100% accurate, they would not make for proof.

Elections, opinion polls and surveys do not prove that something is a good idea

What elections, opinion polls and surveys give you is evidence about what people think about something. They do not prove that something is a good idea. Does the fact that 52% of British people voted in a referendum to leave the EU prove that leaving the EU is a good idea? No; it proves that, on June 23rd 2016, leaving the EU was slightly more popular with British voters than remaining in the EU. If you want to prove that leaving the EU was a good idea, you must show, in much more detail than that, how the benefits of doing so outweigh the costs.

What most people believe, or want to do, may or may not be the right thing to believe or the best thing to do. The debater's job is to **prove** that it is the right or best thing, and simply citing popularity through the medium of elections, referenda, surveys or opinion polls is not proof. When, in 1922, the Irish parliament voted in favour of a treaty of separation from Britain which involved several compromises, Eammon De Valera, who did not approve of the compromises, said, 'The people do not have the right to choose wrong.' Well, actually, they do. But that doesn't stop them being wrong.

To sum up:

- No more entering opinion polls into the search bar when you're preparing for a debate.
- Rely instead on arguments about costs and benefits.
- If the opposition use the argument from democratic majority, swiftly dismiss it by saying something like, 'It may be the case that x has majority support, however, it remains a bad idea because ...' and get back to the main arguments.

5 Argument by authority

'Hannah, tidy up your bedroom.'

'Why?'

'Because it's so untidy you can't find anything in it.'

'But Dad, I'm the only one who has to find things in it, and I know where everything is.'

'It's unhygienic, it's a health hazard.'

'I haven't had a day off school sick in two years.'

'Your sister's is much tidier.'

'I'm not my sister.'

'I hate looking at it.'

'Don't go in there then.'

'Just tidy up your bedroom.'

'Why?'

'Because I'm your Dad and I say so!'

Have you ever had an argument like that? Yes, I thought so. As the parent of a teenager, I've had it myself a few times.

Analyse the arguments you have in daily life in terms of logical fallacies

It's a useful exercise sometimes to analyse the arguments you have in daily life in terms of logical fallacies (though probably not a good idea to do this while you're actually having them, if you don't want to annoy the other person even more than you already have). Let's look at this argument. At first, it progresses through argument and rebuttal, Dad putting arguments, Hannah rebutting them. If I was Dad's debating coach, I would suggest that, while his arguments are both strong and varied, he gives up rather too easily, moving on to a new argument every time he meets rebuttal rather than responding to the rebuttal with a reinforcement of the argument. But it's hard to remember these things when you've had a bad day at work, you're tired, and the dishwasher has broken down again.

Dad's last argument, though, is much weaker, because he essentially gives no reasons for Hannah tidying up her bedroom other than his own position of authority in the family. While it is sometimes necessary for everybody's well-being in a family, a school or wider society for a parent, teacher or police officer to exert their authority without having to explain themselves, this kind of argument - the **argument by authority** - will not win you any points in a debate. The argument by authority is similar to the **argument by democratic majority** we covered above, in that it reaches for something or someone outside the terms of the argument to close down the debate.

Citing an authority does not prove anything

How might it be used in a debate, and how could you rebut it?

In a debate on the motion 'This house would ban private schools', an opposition speaker says:

'It would be wrong to ban private schools because the United Nations Declaration of Human Rights says that parents have the right to decide how their children should be educated.'

How should you rebut this example of argument by authority?

How about this?

'Why should we listen to what the UN says? They're under the control of corrupt leaders in the US and Russia.'

Bad rebuttal. Why? You're guilty of the *ad hominem*, playing the player not the ball, which we discussed above. Don't attack the authority; attack what it says. You can do this even while respecting the authority.

So, try this instead:

'The framers of that declaration had the most admirable intentions, and it has been an inspiration for many vital campaigns. However, they did not foresee the way in which the right for parents to choose their children's education can be abused in countries where private education gives children whose parents who can afford it an unfair advantage. Having the right to educate your son at Eton is a meaningless right for the vast majority of British people, when it costs £40,000 a year and the median household income is £28,000.'

To sum up:

- Simply citing an authority does not prove anything.
- If your opponent cites an authority at you, no matter how admirable the authority:
  - Respect whatever expertise the authority has.
  - Point out the flaws in what the authority says.

6 Introducing irrelevant issues

'Hannah, tidy up your bedroom.'

'Why?'

'Because it's so untidy you can't find anything in it.'

'Maybe, but you forgot to pick me up from hockey practice last Tuesday and I had to take the bus home in the dark and Mum had a go at you about how dangerous it was for me to come home in the dark so why should I listen to you going on about my bedroom?'

Hannah's criticism of her Dad's failure to remember his chauffeuring duties is well supported and powerful. Unfortunately, it has nothing to do with the issue at hand; the tidiness of her bedroom. She hasn't addressed her Dad's argument in favour of tidying up her bedroom, instead moving the debate on to a completely irrelevant issue. By avoiding the central issue, she has lost the debate.

This fallacy is sometimes known as '**Whataboutery**'. This is because debaters who use it often begin with the phrase 'What about...'. To give some examples:

'The use of homophobic language should be made illegal because it legitimises violence against gay people.'

'What about racist language? Shouldn't that be made illegal?'

'GCSEs should be abolished because they create excessive stress for teenagers.'

'What about the stress caused by competitive posting on social media? Why aren't you addressing that?'

'Meat should be taxed because the production of meat contributes to climate change.'

'What about air travel? Why not tax that?'

How should you respond to 'whata-boutery'?

How should you respond to 'whataboutery'? One problem is that the issues raised (like Hannah's Dad's life-threatening forgetfulness) are often very real and important ones. However, you need to recall that they are not the issue that the debate is about. So, agree (briefly) that racism, bodyshaming on Whats App, air travel and not picking up your daughter from hockey practice are bad things, but then remind your opponent that they are not what the debate is about.

To sum up:

- Only introduce issues that are relevant to the motion
- If your opponent introduces irrelevant issues, don't engage with those issues; simply point out that they are not relevant to the debate in hand, and then return to the central issues of the debate in hand.

7 Equating correlation to causation

These are long words, and you may not know what they mean (or maybe you do).

In case you don't:

- **Correlation** means one thing following another.
- **Causation** means one thing causing another.
- **Equating** means assuming two things are the same.

Another, perhaps easier, way of expressing this logical fallacy is as follows:

The fact that A is followed by, or happens at the same time as, B does not prove that B is caused by A.

In your last Maths test you got 90%, your best ever result. You also wore red socks that day. You've got another Maths test tomorrow. How should you ensure you get 90% again? Obvious! Forget revision - just wear red socks!

Forget revision - just wear red socks!

Of course, most people aren't that stupid. But you do see variations on this logical fallacy used in debates.

For example, in a debate on the motion 'This house would ban violent computer games', the proposition argue:

'Violent computer games have never been more popular. At the same time, levels of knife crime amongst young people have never been higher. We need to ban these games now to keep our children safe!'

Knife crime is indisputably a bad thing. Its growth may be happening at the same time as a growth in downloads of violent computer games. But that doesn't, in itself, prove that violent computer games cause knife crime. To do that, you would have to find specific examples of acts of violence that were directly inspired by computer games.

So what should you say to rebut this? You can start by pointing out the logical fallacy:

'Horrific though knife crime is, you have not provided any evidence that it is connected with the use of violent computer games.'

Or, you can turn the connection between the two factors round so that the correlation works in your favour:

'Millions of young people play violent computer games every day, and only a tiny minority engage in acts of violence; this is surely compelling evidence that playing these games is harmless.'

To sum up:

- One thing being followed by, or happening at the same time as, another thing does not mean that the second thing is caused by the first.
- If your opponent tries to use this argument, expose the lack of connection between the two factors.

One thing being followed by another thing does not mean that the second thing is caused by the first

8 Excessive demand

'I had my first ever German lesson today.'

'What's the teacher like?'

'Completely useless! I just watched a German film without subtitles and I couldn't understand a word of what anyone was saying!'

That's a bit harsh, isn't it? However keen you might be to learn the language, even the most brilliant German teacher ever might need a little more time than an hour to get you fluent. But you still see this unfair tactic being used in debating, often in rebuttal.

Let's take an example.

The motion is: 'This house would ban single use plastic.' A speaker for the opposition makes this point of information:

'We need to reduce our carbon emissions to zero by 2025 to

prevent catastrophic climate change. Simply banning single use plastic will not achieve this, so it is a pointless measure.'

The speaker here is making **the best the enemy of the good**. However admirable the 2025 goal may be, she is demanding more from the proposition than they can reasonably be expected to provide within the terms of the motion, just like the German student and her teacher.

Don't make the best the enemy of the good

How should the proposition respond?

'The 2025 target is an excellent one, and one we support. It is true that banning single use plastic will not achieve that target by itself, but it will greatly assist the achievement of that target. Here is how it will help ...'

To sum up:

- If you are rebutting the proposition, don't attack their action for not achieving something it cannot reasonably be expected to achieve.
- If the opposition attack you on this basis, gently but firmly lead them back to what the motion is really about.

9 False analogy

Analogy means explaining something by comparing it to something else. It can be a very helpful tool for understanding things. Teachers use it a lot. The trouble is that the thing you're explaining and the thing you're comparing it to are not the same; in some ways they will be different. When they're so different that they can't fairly be compared, the analogy becomes a false analogy.

Let's look at an example.

In a debate on the motion, 'This house would abolish exam result league tables for schools', an opposition speaker says:

'Imagine if we got rid of league tables for the Premier League, and all the teams just played for fun; who would want to watch football then?'

She is making an analogy between schools and football teams. However, schools are actually not much like football teams. All that they have in common is that they are both ranked in league tables. The only thing a football team does is play football, and the only purpose of playing football is to win. No one would want to watch a football team that didn't play to win. Schools, however, do many more things for students than prepare them for exams: they teach them social skills; they offer them extra-curricular activities (such as football, and debating); they teach values like respect for others; they aim to bring out the best in all their students, whatever their ability. No one would want to go to a school where the students were treated like players in a Premier League football team, rewarded when they produced results that sent the team up the league table, dropped when they didn't.

How to respond to this false analogy?

'I agree with the speaker. Football would be very boring if there were no league tables. But schools are not football teams, because …'

Schools are not football teams

To sum up:

- If you are using an analogy, make sure the two terms are similar enough for it to work.
- If your opponent uses an analogy, look for the ways in which the two terms do not connect, and try to prize them apart.

10 Misidentified problem

This, from a speech in favour of the motion 'This house would ban single-use plastic':

'We use plastic cups for water in our school lunch room and they're really annoying because they keep tipping over and spilling. That's why reusable water bottles are better.'

What's wrong with it? It's missing the point, that's what. The central argument against single-use plastic is the damage it does to the environment by being non-biodegradable. Badly designed plastic cups that tip over have nothing to do with that. After all, it would be quite possible to design plastic cups that don't tip over. It's probably been done already, and the school just needs to buy some in. But doing that would only increase the use of single-use plastic.

If you're arguing for the proposition, you need to find the central problem that the motion is addressing, and focus rigorously on that one problem; here, it's the environmental damage that single-use plastic causes. Otherwise, you undermine the strength of your own case.

It's possible to make the same mistake when you're the opposition, by identifying a problem with the proposition which is not relevant to the motion. So, for example, a speaker opposing the motion 'This house would introduce a 20 mile per hour speed limit in cities' might say:

'This will take up a lot of police time arresting people who break the speed limit, and those police won't be able to prevent knife crime, and knife crime will go up.'

Any law is going to need to be enforced, and that is going to take up some resources. The only question is whether it is a good law; this is what the opposition needs to address.

If your opponent is guilty of **misidentifying the problem**, point out that the problem they have identified, while real, is not relevant to the motion, and steer the argument back to the main problem.

'It may be the case that water bottles would work better in your lunch room than plastic cups. However, while making plastic cups illegal might solve that problem, it would create other, much bigger problems, such as …'

'Enforcing the speed limit will take up some resources. However, those resources will be well spent, because of the benefits the new law will bring. These are …'

To sum up:

- If you are the proposition, find the essential problem the action of the motion is trying to solve and focus on that.
- If you are the opposition, find the essential problem the action of the motion will cause and focus on that.
- If your opponent misses the essential problem, point out (not least to the judges) what they have done, and return to the essential problem.

11 Misidentified solution

This is the sister, as it were, of the misidentified problem. It supports the action of the motion by attributing to it benefits which are either irrelevant or trivial, when the speaker should be focusing on the essential, substantial benefits. It's a bad argument that can only really be made by the proposition.

So, for example, speaking in favour of the motion: 'This house would make voting in General Elections compulsory':

'If voting was compulsory, there would be more votes to count, and more people would be needed to count them. This would provide extra income to the counters, which would boost the economy.'

What's wrong with this? It misses the essential, substantial point of the motion, which is about the benefits to the democratic process of making voting compulsory. As well as being irrelevant to the development of democracy, the benefits of the extra employment for counters would be trivial; elections usually only take place once every five years, and counting only takes place over one night, so the income generated would be very small.

How should you respond to the misidentified solution if you are the opposition?

One thing you should not do is mirror the misidentified solution with a misidentified problem of your own. In the compulsory voting example, that would mean complaining about the cost to the taxpayer of printing extra ballot papers / hiring extra counters. This would trap you in the same error of irrelevance and triviality.

Instead, point out how the solution the proposition have given is irrelevant and / or trivial. Do this briefly and briskly, though. As soon as possible, steer the debate back to the essential solution implied in the motion, and show how it is flawed. If you spend too long attacking weak arguments, you will not show your own strength; but if you are unafraid to attack your opponent at their strongest point, you will be able to demonstrate the strength of your own arguments to the judges.

If you spend too long attacking weak arguments, you will not show your own strength

So, you might say:

'The benefit of extra employment for vote counters would be extremely small, as that employment would only be available on one night every five years. The harm of making voting compulsory would be much greater. The element of compulsion would create resentment, and this would mean …'

To sum up:

- Identify the essential and substantial benefit(s) of the action proposed by the motion, and focus on it / them rigorously.
- If your opponent misidentifies the solution, briefly point this out, and return to attacking the essential and substantial solution implied by the motion.

12 Slippery slope

'Jack, I've booked a dentist's appointment for you on Tuesday.'

'When?'

'Nine o'clock.'

'But, Mum, then I'll have to miss Maths!'

'It's all right, I'll email the school and get permission for you to be absent, you won't get into trouble.'

'But if I miss Maths, I'll fall behind … and if I fall behind my marks will drop … and if my marks drop I won't get as good a GCSE grade … and if my GCSE grades drop I won't be able to get into university … and then I won't be able to get a job … and then I'll end up living on the streets … and someone might attack me one night … and then I'll be dead before I'm twenty …'

See what Jack was doing there? He started with a small problem (missing Maths) and assumed that it would inevitably lead to a much bigger problem (being murdered). He implied a whole set of inevitable consequences from the action of missing Maths, none of which he proved to be inevitable.

Missing Maths doesn't lead to being murdered

This is known as the **slippery slope** argument. It posits an inevitable progression towards an extreme consequence for an action without proving that this consequence is inevitable or even likely. It is a bad argument that will almost always be made by the opposition.

Say the motion is: 'This house would abolish GCSEs.' An opposition speaker says:

'If we abolish GCSEs, students in Years 10 and 11 will have no motivation to study. As a result, they will pay no attention in class. No one will learn anything, and students will leave school without basic literacy and numeracy skills. They will not be able to find work, and will have no choice but to turn to crime, and the murder rate will go up.'

Point out the implausibility of the harm

This starts with a strong argument against abolishing public exams: the benefit of the level of focus and motivation these exams inspire in students, and the harm of losing that focus and motivation. Unfortunately, it then goes on to undermine that argument by greatly exaggerating the harm.

What could the speaker have done better?

Focus on a realistic, likely harm from the action proposed for the motion, for which there is some evidence. In this case, she could have said:

'Once the pressure of public exams is removed, many students lose motivation to study. There is an example of this is at A-Level. Students who have been given unconditional offers for university often work much less hard, and as a result achieve lower grades than they are capable of.'

This is a much stronger argument, because it is more plausible. If Jack had just told his Mum he'd rather not miss Maths because they've got a big test coming up soon, so could she please see if the dentist has any appointments on a Saturday, she would be more likely to listen to him.

How should you respond if your opponent uses the slippery slope argument?

It enables you to avoid having to deal with the more likely harm, because you can focus on rebutting the less likely harm. Point out the implausibility of the harm and the lack of evidence offered for it, and then steer the argument back to your terms:

'While some students may temporarily lose some motivation in the absence of public exams, the great majority will still be mature enough to see that it is not in their interests to disengage from school. It is highly unlikely that any but a very small minority would disengage to the extent that they would leave school with no skills, or will turn to crime. It is actually more likely that students will be more motivated, as lessons will be more interesting and stimulating once they no longer have to focus on boring, repetitive drilling for exams …'

To sum up:

- If you're the opposition, don't exaggerate the harms that the action proposed by the motion will bring.
- Focus on likely harms which are easier to prove.
- If your opponent exaggerates harms, point out how unlikely they are and then return to the benefits of your proposed action.

Heroic trailblazers versus nasty misogynists

13 False dichotomy

The motion is 'This house would make it compulsory for 50% of places on science courses at university to be offered to women.' The speaker for the proposition says:

'Either you support this motion, or you are saying that women are incapable of studying science.'

She is polarising. That is, she is trying to divide the argument into two extreme positions: on the one hand, heroic trailblazers like her, who will liberate women from their shackles and enable them to achieve dazzling new scientific discoveries, on the other, nasty misogynists who think that women should not be educated but should stay at home cooking, cleaning and looking after the children so that their husbands have more time to find a cure for cancer. In doing this, she is setting up a **false dichotomy**. A **dichotomy** is the division of a case into two mutually incompatible parts, with no possibility of compromise: either you're one thing, or you're the other - there's no middle ground.

It is very rare that a debate motion is as absolute as this. You will usually put yourself in a much stronger position if you concede that there is some common ground between you and your opponent. So, with this motion, better to say:

'The opposition says that the current system is fair and equal, and puts no barriers in the way of women scientists. We disagree, because …'

Here you are conceding that the opposition do share your intentions of encouraging women to study science; they're just going about it the wrong way. This makes you look much more reasonable, and makes your criticism of their plan for achieving the goal you share much more plausible.

If your opponent uses **false dichotomy**, don't get angry at the way in which you have implicitly been pushed to an extreme position. Instead, gently but firmly move the focus of the debate back to the middle ground, and show how you are on the right side of that middle ground:

'We do not think that women should not study science. We think women should be encouraged to study science, and that women scientists should be respected and celebrated. Our concern is that if women are seen to have only achieved their place on a course to fulfil a quota, then they will not inspire this respect in the same way as if they had achieved the place by their own merits …'

To sum up:

- Don't divide the case into irreconcilable extremes. Very few cases divide in this way.
- Instead, aim for the middle ground and find the point of clash there.
- If your opponent uses false dichotomy, rebut the false division, and gently but firmly steer the debate back to the middle ground.

Aim for the middle ground

Why is this chapter useful for life?

This skill of analysing arguments is (once again) a very useful skill for life, as you are constantly, every day, being presented with arguments, reasons why you should believe something or why you should do something. Some of these arguments are very good; some are very bad; some are downright dishonest. Once you are aware of these fallacies, you are much less likely to be fooled.

What have we learnt in this chapter?

1. Thirteen logical fallacies ☐
2. What's wrong with them ☐
3. How to avoid using them ☐
4. How to rebut your opponents when they use them ☐

Do this before you read the next chapter

- Watch or listen to a political discussion programme, such as the BBC's Question Time, or BBC Radio 4's Today programme, and see how many examples of logical fallacies you can find (there will be lots ...).

- Do the same thing with opinion / editorial articles in either printed newspapers or online.

- In your debating club, have your coach write the titles of all these fallacies on pieces of card. Everyone picks a card. They then have to give a short speech on a topic using the fallacy they have been given. Other members of the club have to spot what the fallacy is and rebut it.

CHAPTER 8

How to win a debate

In this chapter we'll be learning about how judges decide who has won a debate.

Debating is a competitive activity. You should be in it to win it.

But how do you win?

In football, netball and hockey you win by scoring more goals than the opposition. Anyone watching the game (provided they can count) knows who has won as soon as the final whistle is blown.

That isn't the case in debating.

The people who decide who has won the debate are the **judges**. In a major competition, you are likely to have at least two per debate, though in smaller competitions you may have only one. One important thing to understand is that the judges' decision is a **qualitative** one. That means that marking a debate is not like marking a Maths or Science exam, where you accumulate marks by getting right answers. It's more like marking an English or History exam, where you're awarded marks for demonstrating certain skills across a whole essay.

What are those skills? What are judges looking for?

In one sense, there is only one skill needed to win a debate. The judging criteria can be summed up in one sentence:

Which team has made the more persuasive case?

Everything you do as a debater should be focused towards that one aim; persuading listeners to agree with your side of the case. And remember, the listeners who will decide if you have won the debate are the judges.

But how do the judges decide who has made the more persuasive case?

They will be breaking down the debate into the key skills of debating, all of which help to make your case more persuasive, and seeing how well you display your mastery of each of them. They will be asking questions of your speeches and points of information, to see if you are using these key skills.

The people who decide who has won the debate are the judges

Focus on the skills

What are the key skills, and what questions will the judges be asking?

1 Reasoning and evidence

This skill shows you can construct a convincing case.

- How well has the motion been defined?
- Have the arguments been clearly and logically constructed?
- Have appropriate examples and evidence been used?
- Is everything said relevant to the motion?
- Are the speakers guilty of any logical fallacies?

2 Listening and response

This skill shows you understand the other side of the case and can rebut it.

- How effective and thorough is rebuttal of previous speakers?
- Are points of information precise, concise, timely, focused and relevant?
- Has the point of clash been identified and used effectively?

3 Organisation and prioritisation

This skill shows you can present your case in the clearest possible way.

- Are there the right number of arguments (usually three per speech)?
- Are they organised effectively, with the strongest coming first?
- Are the arguments divided effectively between speakers?
- Is time used effectively, i.e.
  - approximately one minute per argument
  - one minute for rebuttal
  - one minute for taking points of information
  - speaking right up to the signal for the end of speaking time?

4 Expression and delivery

This skill shows you can speak in a convincing way. (NB this is not part of the mark scheme in BP; however, doing it effectively will still make a good impression on BP judges.)

- Do the speakers speak clearly and audibly?
- Do they vary their pace and tone for effect?
- Do they use eye contact?
- Do they keep dependence on notes to a minimum?
- Do they sound as if they care about what they are saying?
- Do they (where appropriate) use humour effectively?

5 Team work and roles

This skill shows you make a strong case by working together as a team, and making the most of the role you have been given.

- Do the speakers support to and refer to each other?
- Do they avoid contradicting or repeating each other?
- Do they fulfil the particular tasks of their roles effectively, i.e.

  Prop 1: defining the motion and introducing the case

  Prop 2, Opp 1, Opp 2: rebutting previous speakers and building the case further

  Prop 3 and Opp 3 (BP only): finding an extension to the case set out by the first two speakers on their side.

  Summary speakers (Extended Mace and BP only):

  - summing up their side's case
  - summing up their opponents' case and rebutting it
  - responding to floor speeches (Extended Mace only)
  - finding the point of clash and showing how their side have won the debate
  - avoiding introducing new material

Judges help you

A judge will have all these things in mind when she is watching a debate.

Where you have more than one judge in a debate, they will make notes separately, and confer out of earshot of the debaters before they give their verdict.

Although judges are people who, er, judge you, they are also people who help you.

How?

Like teachers returning homework, judges will almost always give feedback before they deliver their verdict. Listen very carefully to this feedback, taking notes if possible; it will tell you what you are doing well, and what you need to work on. If they don't give feedback, or if there is part of the feedback that you do not understand, it is quite acceptable to ask them politely if they would mind telling you more. However, be very careful not to do or say anything that could be interpreted as challenging their verdict. Judges are human and can make mistakes, but it is a fundamental point of debating etiquette that, while you may respectfully ask for clarification, a judge's verdict once given is final.

What have we learnt in this chapter?

1. What the key skills debaters have to display are ☐
2. How judges arrive at their verdict ☐
3. How to use judges' feedback ☐

Do this before you read the next chapter

- In your debating club, have one group stage a debate while the rest watch it, acting as judges. Practise taking notes like a judge, discussing your verdict with others, and giving feedback, in order to get inside the experience of a judge.
- Do the same with a recorded debate online.

CHAPTER 9

The Big Ideas

In this chapter we'll be learning about different ways of seeing the world, and how the clash between them is behind many debates.

'Of course people should be able to hire whomever they want for a job.'

'Of course the government should provide free health care and education.'

'Of course anybody should be allowed to live in any country they want.'

I hope you've realised by now that there are almost no 'of courses.' That's pretty much the point of debating; almost everything is up for discussion and disagreement, almost nothing is ever finally settled. And yet, it's surprising how often people assume that their way of seeing the world is the only possible way, and that anyone who disagrees with them is either evil or stupid. That's usually because they haven't examined the assumptions behind their beliefs. Once you examine the assumptions behind your beliefs, you will soon see that they are just that, assumptions rather than absolute truths, and that there are almost always opposite, and equally valid, assumptions opposing them.

Almost nothing is ever finally proved

What are the assumptions behind the 'of courses' above?

'Of course people should be able to hire whomever they want for a job.'

Freedom to do what you want is more important than freedom from unfair treatment.

'Of course the government should provide free health care and education.'

Providing the necessities of life is the responsibility of the state, not the individual.

'Of course anybody should be allowed to live in any country they want.'

Diversity is a higher good than stability.

Any of those assumptions could be switched around to make the opposite case. Suddenly, there's no 'of course'. That's one of the (many) great things about debating; it makes you question everything.

So, in this chapter, we're going to be learning about three of the most important Big Ideas. Big Ideas are the fundamental issues which lie deep below debate motions. If you can understand what Big Ideas are and how they work, you will see the motion in a new way, and you will also be able to take control of the debate and steer it in a way that favours your side. Big Ideas are concerned with two opposite values, at opposite ends of a line. Think of them as being like two people at different ends of a tug of war. Sometimes the rope pulls one way; sometimes it pulls the other. Your job as a debater is to decide which end of the rope your side of the motion lies on, and to keep pulling in that direction.

Your job is to keep pulling in your direction

The Big Ideas we're going to be looking at are:

- Freedom to vs Freedom from
- Social liberalism vs social conservatism
- Neo-liberalism vs social democracy

1 Freedom to vs Freedom from

What is the difference between **Freedom to** and **Freedom from**?

If you value **freedom to** above all, you think people should be allowed to make their own choices, but should also accept the consequences of those choices. You accept that there is a risk in this approach. People might make bad choices, which might damage them, and might also damage others, but you believe that this is a risk worth taking, because it is more important to be **free to** do what you choose than to be **free from** the consequences of your choices. You might also argue that **freedom to** works better than **freedom from**, because people tend to make better choices when they have ownership of those choices and the consequences.

If you value **freedom from** above all, you think people's choices should be regulated to protect them and others. You accept that this means sacrificing some liberty, but you believe that this is a worthwhile sacrifice in order to protect individuals and society at large. You are likely to believe that **freedom from** works better than liberty, because too much freedom to tends to lead to chaos and injustice, with the strong ruling over the weak.

How can you apply this Big Idea to analysing a motion?

Not all Big Ideas apply to all motions. The **Freedom to** vs **Freedom from** Big Idea applies best to motions which are about whether people's behaviour should be controlled or not.

Here are some motions it works well with, and how to apply it:

1. **This house would legalise drugs**

   Freedom to sides with the proposition; **freedom from** sides with the opposition.

   Freedom to says:

   - People should decide whether to harm themselves with drugs or not; it is a private decision, and not the business of the government. (**Freedom to** is a higher value than **freedom from**).
   - People are going to take drugs anyway. By making it illegal, you create crime and criminal gangs. (**Freedom to** works better than **freedom from**).

   Freedom from says:

   - People are likely to take drugs, but at least making them illegal makes it less likely and thus minimises the harm. (**Freedom from** protects people; the law keeps them free from the danger of drugs).
   - The free taking of drugs will be disastrous for health and productivity. (**Freedom from** works better than **freedom to**).

2. **This house would ban hate speech**

   Freedom to sides with the proposition; **freedom from** sides with the opposition.

   Freedom to says:

   - Free and open debate is an essential part of a healthy society. The risk of someone being offended is the price we pay for an open society. (The **freedom to** say what you think is a higher good than **freedom from** offence.)
   - Hate is better challenged in open debate than by being driven underground, which allows haters to present themselves as martyrs. (**Freedom to** works better than **freedom from**.)

   Freedom from says:

   - A healthy society is one where mutual respect is practised. This requires some censorship of unacceptable views. (**Freedom from** disrespect and offence is a higher good than **freedom to** say what you like.)
   - By enshrining mutually respectful speech in the law, you will make people behave more respectfully. (**Freedom from** works better than **freedom to**.)

Which works better? Freedom To or Freedom From?

3. **This house would impose a 20 mph speed limit in cities.**

Freedom to sides with the opposition; **freedom from** sides with the proposition.

Freedom to says:

- Provided people drive safely, they should be allowed to drive at whatever speed they like. (**Freedom to** do what you choose is a higher good than **freedom from** the occasional abuse of this freedom).
- Having a low speed limit will make drivers angry and frustrated and therefore likely to drive more dangerously. (**Freedom from** works worse than **freedom to**).

Freedom from says:

- Keeping the roads safe, and cities less polluted, is more important than letting drivers have their way. (**Freedom from** the consequences of other people's selfish choices is a higher good than **freedom to** make those choices).
- The speed limit may encourage more people to give up their cars and walk or cycle instead, which will make for a healthier and greener city. (**Freedom from** works better than **freedom to**).

Ideas are based very firmly on values

2 Neo-liberalism vs social democracy

What are **neo-liberalism** and **social democracy?** What do neo-liberals and social democrats believe?

They are both ideas you might learn about in an Economics lesson, as they are concerned with how resources are allocated and distributed. However, far from being mere mathematical abstractions, they are based very firmly on values.

What are those values?

For neo-liberals, the **individual** is more important than the **community**, and **liberty** is a higher good than **equality**. For social democrats, the **community** is more important than the **individual**, and **equality** is a higher good than **liberty**. In the **freedom to vs freedom from** clash we discussed above, neo-liberals would most often come down on the side of **freedom to**, and social democrats would most often come down on the side of **freedom from**. Both sides think their approach is both fairer and more effective.

Now let's see how those values are applied, both in terms of economic principles and of practical measures.

Neo-liberalism

Principles

- Everyone is responsible for themselves
- The less government, the better
- People have the right to keep whatever they have earned by their work
- People work hardest and most productively when they are left alone to make their own decisions
- People should accept the consequences of their decisions and not expect the government to look after them
- Competition between businesses is the best guarantee of efficiency and good customer service
- Inequality is a good thing, as it motivates people to work harder

Practical measures

- Low taxes
- Low government spending
- Minimum regulation
- Introduce competition wherever possible

Everyone is responsible for themselves

Or

We are responsible for each other

Social democracy

Principles

- We are all responsible for each other; the strong have a moral duty to help the weak
- People work best and most productively when they work with support from outside
- Government can be a force for good, protecting the weak against the strong
- Government intervention can make the economy work better, because the government acts in the interests of all the people
- Inequality is a bad thing, as it breeds division and resentment
- Collaboration is better than competition

Practical measures

- High taxes, with the wealthiest paying the most
- High government spending
- Social benefits, such as health, education, pensions etc. funded by taxation and provided to all free at the point of use
- Some parts of the economy run by the government in the interests of the whole of society
- High levels of regulation, to ensure that businesses look after their employees and customers

Now we have an understanding of the values of the two different sides, let's look at how they might clash in some debate motions.

1. **This house would abolish university tuition fees.**

   Social democracy sides with the proposition; **neo-liberalism** sides with the opposition.

   A **social democrat** argues:

   - University education should be available to everyone who has qualified for it academically; no one should be excluded because they cannot afford it. **(Inclusion is better than competition.)**
   - Children of rich parents sometimes have all their fees paid by their parents and never have to worry about repaying them, while other equally able students are saddled with debt for years afterwards. **(Money should not buy privilege.)**
   - A well educated workforce is a benefit to the whole of society, so it is in all our interests for the government to invest in education. **(Government intervention works.)**
   - Making distinctions between those who can afford university education and those who can't is divisive and undermines social solidarity. **(Inequality is bad for society.)**

   A **neo-liberal** argues:

   - People only value what they pay for. Subsidising education makes people value it less. **(People should take responsibility for their choices.)**

Education should be available to everyone

Or

People only value what they pay for

Equality or liberty?

- Having a university education is a benefit; graduates earn far more than non-graduates, so it is only fair that people should pay for a university education. **(People should only have what they have earned by their own efforts.)**
- It is a basic human right to be able to bring up your children in the way you choose. Parents who choose to pay their children's tuition fees are only exercising this right. **(Freedom to spend your money how you like is a higher good than freedom from injustice.)**
- Measures such as this can only be funded by higher taxes. Higher taxes damage the economy and cost jobs, to everyone's detriment. **(Neo-liberalism works better than social democracy.)**

2. **This house would introduce a maximum wage**

Social democrats side with the proposition; **neo-liberals** side with the opposition.

A **social democrat** argues:

- It is fair that some people should earn more than others, but incomes at the very top level are beyond what anyone deserves or needs. **(Inequality is an inherently bad thing.)**
- Unlimited incomes promote extreme inequality, which breeds division and resentment. **(Inequality is bad for society.)**
- Extreme wealth gives some individuals disproportionate political power (e.g by donating to political parties, threatening to take their businesses out of the country if they do not get their way etc.) and this is undemocratic. **(We have a greater responsibility to society than to ourselves.)**
- In a more equal society, everyone feels more valued and more connected to each other. **(Equality is an inherently good thing.)**

A **neo-liberal** argues:

- The government has no right to tell people what they can earn. **(The less government intervention, the better.)**
- Introducing a maximum wage disincentivises hard work. **(People work best when rewarded for their work.)**

- Talented individuals will be driven out of the country. **(Social democracy works worse than neo-liberalism.)**
- The very rich benefit society by paying lots of money in taxes and by investing in businesses which provide thousands of jobs. **(Neo-liberalism is more efficient than social democracy.)**

3. **This house would bring the railways into public ownership**

Social democrats support the proposition; **neo-liberals** support the opposition.

A **social democrat** argues:

- Competition may work well in some sectors, but not in the railways. There is not sufficient capacity for competing offers. For example, there is only one track from London to Edinburgh, so there can only be one company running that line. **(Collaboration is better than competition.)**
- Governments are more incentivised and able to take the long term view, investing in maintaining and updating tracks and stations; businesses are only interested in short term profit. **(The state protects our interests better than individuals.)**
- Removing the need for profit and introducing subsidies could bring down fare prices, to everyone's benefit. Cheaper fares would also incentivise people to use public transport more, to the benefit of the environment. **(The state has the right to intervene in society.)**
- Having an efficient, cheap, reliable railway service to carry goods and people around is good for the economy, so it is worth having the government invest in it. **(Government intervention makes the economy work better.)**

A **neo-liberal** argues:

- Without competition, the people running the railways will become lazy and complacent. **(Competition is a good thing.)**
- Competition will motivate companies to provide the best service and lowest prices. **(Competition works.)**

- Higher public investment in the railways will mean higher taxes, which will discourage businesses and individuals from working harder. **(Taxes should be as low as possible.)**
- Being able to travel is a benefit, and people should expect to pay for it. **(People should take responsibility for their own choices.)**

Here are some more motions which could easily break on neoliberal vs social democratic lines:

- **This house would privatise the NHS.**
- **This house would introduce a flat tax *(see the next chapter for an explanation of what a flat tax is)*.**
- **This house would cut benefits.**

Knowing about neo-liberalism and social democracy is also very useful when following current affairs (as all debaters should). Often there are arguments about economic measures. Both sides present their proposals as being simply common sense. Seeing what economic assumptions (and ultimately what value systems) people are using helps you to evaluate their arguments better.

Let's give the last word on neo-liberalism and social democracy to two characters in a very well known play: *An Inspector Calls* by J.B. Priestley. You may have studied, or be studying, this play; it is very often taught in UK schools. In many ways it's a debate between neo-liberal and social democratic ideas. Mr Birling, a wealthy industrialist, represents neo-liberal ideas when he says:

... a man has to mind his own business and look after himself and his own ...

while the Inspector, whose job it is to reveal uncomfortable truths about the Birling family, puts the social democratic case when he says:

We are members of one body. We are responsible for one another.

Priestley was firmly on the side of social democracy, and makes sure that the Inspector wins the debate in the play. But you have to make your own mind up.

Both sides present their proposals as being simply common sense

3 Social liberalism vs social conservatism

What is the difference between a **social liberal** and a **social conservative**?

A **social liberal** believes:

- We live in the world as individuals, each different and distinct.
- We should be allowed to make our own choices about how we live; where we live; what we believe; whom we love.
- Identities shared across national borders such as race, gender and sexuality are more important than identities based around nationality or region.
- Change, variety and fluidity are higher goods than familiarity, similarity and community.
- A country or region has a responsibility to accept and welcome incomers, and to allow them to preserve their identity.
- Tolerance of different ways of life is a higher good than conformity to shared ways of life.

Change or familiarity?

A **social conservative** believes:

- We live in the world as part of a community defined by common values and practices.
- We should respect these common values and practices, and prioritise them over our own personal desires.
- National or regional identities are more important than transnational identities based on race, gender or sexuality.
- Familiarity, similarity and community are higher goods than change, variety and fluidity.
- Incomers to a country or region have a responsibility to adapt to their new home's way of doing things, abandoning their own values if necessary.
- Conformity to shared values is a higher good than tolerance of diversity.

How can you apply this clash of values to debate motions?

1. **This house would abolish immigration controls**

   Social liberalism sides with the proposition; **social conservatism** sides with the opposition.

A **social liberal** argues:

- Our economy depends on immigrants; they tend to be hard working and willing to do jobs natives wouldn't do. They are also more likely to be young and fit, contributing to the country through taxes rather than using health care and benefits. **(Social liberalism works better than social conservatism.)**
- Immigration has enriched our society culturally. Britain is a more diverse and exciting place because of it. **(Variety and change are better than familiarity and uniformity; we should adapt to welcome incomers.)**
- We have a moral responsibility to welcome people less fortunate than ourselves. **(Our responsibility is to the whole of humanity, not just our national community.)**

A **social conservative** argues:

- Immigrants drive down wages and take jobs from local workers. **(Social conservatism works better than social liberalism.)**
- Immigration has caused Britain to lose its identity; we no longer have common values. **(Familiarity and uniformity are better than change and variety; incomers should adapt to a community rather than the other way round.)**
- We need to look after our own country first. **(Our responsibility is to our immediate community, not the whole of humanity.)**

2. **This house would make it compulsory for all schools to teach that gay relationships are equal to straight relationships.**

Social liberalism backs the proposition; **social conservatism** backs the opposition.

A **social liberal** argues:

- Diverse sexualities and ways of living enrich our society, and should be celebrated at all ages and all levels of society. **(Diversity is a higher good than uniformity.)**
- What we teach in our schools defines who we are as a society, and we want to be a tolerant society. **(Tolerance is a higher good than conformity.)**

- The rights of gay students to express their sexuality freely are more important than the rights of religious groups who teach that homosexuality is wrong. **(Identity based on individual lifestyle is more important than identity based on shared tradition.)**

A **social conservative** argues:

- The family is the bedrock of society, and the best way to bring up children; there is nothing wrong with celebrating traditional ways of living above how a minority of people live. **(Social cohesion is a higher good than diversity.)**
- It is not right to impose values on communities who may not share those values, e.g. making a school in a majority Muslim area teach gay rights. **(Community values are more important than universal values.)**
- Religious objections to teaching gay rights should be respected, because the great world faiths have a greater depth and strength than contemporary fashions. **(Tradition is more valuable than modernity.)**

3. This house would ban the wearing of the niqab in public

Social conservatism supports the proposition; **social liberalism** supports the opposition.

A **social conservative** argues:

Diversity or solidarity?

- Women who wear the niqab shut themselves off from mainstream British society. **(Incomers have a responsibility to adapt to the shared values of the society they come into.)**
- The wearing of the niqab is a public demonstration of the oppression of women. **(Sub-groups within society do not have the right to promote values that contradict those of the community as a whole; social cohesion is a higher good than tolerance.)**
- Britain's culture is based on different values to those of Islam; public celebrations of Islamic culture threaten our national identity. **(The preservation of shared values is a higher good than diversity.)**

Tradition or modernity?

A **social liberal** argues:

- People should be allowed to dress how they like. **(Acceptance of diversity is a higher good than conformity to shared values.)**
- Banning ways of dress associated with certain ethnic groups opens the door to racism. **(Tolerance is the highest good.)**
- British values are in fact based on tolerance and openness, and we should therefore accept and celebrate different ways of dressing. **(An open society is a good society.)**

I think it's fair to say that most British people under the age of 25, particularly those either at university or likely to go to university - in other words most debaters - are more likely to identify with the values of social liberalism than with those of social conservatism. That makes it all the more important to understand that there is another way to see the world, which is not necessarily stupid or evil.

I hope you can see now how useful the Big Ideas are. They apply to a surprising number of debates. Once you start seeing motions through the lens of a Big Idea, you can analyse them much more effectively and create better arguments. During a Big Ideas debate, keep the Big Idea in mind, constantly pulling the rope of the discussion back towards your end of the clash, talking up the values of your side and exposing the failings of the values of the other side.

What have we learnt in this chapter?

The following Big Ideas:

1. Freedom to vs freedom from ☐
2. Social liberalism vs social conservatism ☐
3. Neo-liberalism vs social democracy ☐
4. The values behind them ☐
5. How they can be used in debates ☐

Do this before you read the next chapter

- Watch or listen to radio or TV programmes which feature political and moral debate (e.g. the BBC's *Question Time*, or BBC Radio 4's *The Moral Maze*.) Analyse the arguments made in terms of Big Ideas.
- Do the same with written opinion pieces in newspapers and magazines / online.
- Take some common debate motions and, discussing together in your debate club, think about how you can analyse them in terms of Big Ideas.

CHAPTER 10

What debaters need to know about the world

In this chapter, we're going to be learning some basic facts all debaters need to know about how the UK is run and about how the economy works.

One of the (many, many) good things about debating is that it not only teaches you how to argue; it also teaches you about the world. You cannot succeed in debating without being well informed about how the world works, and what is happening in it.

We will talk more in Chapter 14 about ways in which you can keep your current affairs information up to date. In this chapter, though, we'll learn about two key areas of knowledge you need to master as a debater, both of which apply to a great many debates:

- **How the UK is run**
- **How the economy works**

Knowing the rules of a game helps you to follow it

1 How the UK is run

If you were watching a football match with someone, and they kept asking you why the players didn't pick up the ball and run with it, you probably wouldn't much respect their opinion on how the teams should play. Knowing the rules of a game helps you to follow it. Similarly, knowing the rules of how Britain is run helps you to have an informed opinion on how it could be run better.

The rules for running a country are known as its **constitution**.

What is the the UK constitution?

The first thing to know about the British constitution is that it doesn't exist.

Other countries, such as the United States, have a written constitution. There are often disagreements about what that written constitution really means, but at least there is one document to which everyone can refer. This has never happened in the UK (and one possible debate is 'This house would introduce a written constitution for the UK'). Instead, the constitution has been determined partly by custom and practice - what everyone has always done and what they're expected to carry on doing - and partly through various documents and by occasional laws, passed as and when they are needed, in no very systematic fashion. The advantage of the unwritten constitution is that it can be flexible and responsive to the changing needs of a changing world; the disadvantage is that difficult situations can arise where no one knows what to do.

What is the point of the monarchy?

The Queen has no power at all

The monarch - at the time of writing Queen Elizabeth II - is the **head of state**. In theory, she is in charge of everything. Her head is on bank notes and coins, issued by Her Majesty's Treasury, and on postage stamps, issued by the Royal Mail. She is Commander-in-Chief of the Armed Forces. When someone is put on trial, they are prosecuted in her name; all criminal cases are 'Regina (Latin for the Queen) vs [name of the defendant]'. We pay taxes to Her Majesty's Revenues and Customs. The government is Her Majesty's Government. The government's programme is announced in the Queen's Speech, given by her, in which every paragraph begins 'My government will ...' Prime Ministers and ministers are appointed by her, and can be dismissed by her. No laws can be passed until she has signed them.

In practice, she has no power at all. Her role is purely symbolic. She is a figurehead, representing the UK at big national events, such as the opening of the 2012 Olympics in London, or commemorations of major anniversaries, or visiting the victims of terrorist attacks or natural disasters.

However, she does have a role in the government of the UK. We will see how as we learn about elections and how governments are formed. If you find yourself taking part in a debate about abolishing the monarchy, remember to focus on this constitutional role, and whether it is best performed by an unelected monarch (who belongs to everyone and is attached to no party) or an elected head of state (who has been chosen by the people). Don't get sidetracked into whether or not the Queen is a nice person, or that rude thing the Duke of Edinburgh said to someone once. This is the *ad hominem* argument (see Chapter 7, Big Fat Fallacies).

How do elections work?

A **General Election** is called when the Queen, on the advice of the Prime Minister, dissolves parliament. Dissolving parliament means that all the Members of Parliament (MPs) are out of a job, and new ones have to be appointed. If existing MPs want to continue being MPs, they are effectively reapplying for their jobs by standing for election.

Under the terms of the Fixed Terms Parliament Act, passed in 2010, this should only happen once every five years. The only way in which an election can happen earlier is when either:

- Two thirds of MPs vote in favour of an early dissolution of parliament (this happened in 2017 and 2019).

or

- The government loses a vote in parliament on the motion 'This house has no confidence in Her Majesty's Government' (often known as a 'confidence motion'). When this happens, 14 days are allowed to see if the leader of a different party in parliament from the one which was governing can form a government. If this does not happen, a General Election is called.

MPs each represent a **constituency.** Britain is divided into 650 constituencies, each with around 70,000 voters in them. In densely populated cities constituencies cover quite a small area; in sparsely populated rural areas they will be much larger. Citizens of the UK and the Commonwealth (the Commonwealth is made up mostly of countries that used to be in the British Empire) who are over the age of 18 and are resident in the UK are allowed to vote in General Elections, though it is not compulsory. Anyone can stand for election in any constituency provided they get the support of at least ten people and put down some money, called a deposit, which they don't get back if they get below a certain percentage of the vote. In practice, most candidates in elections are representing one of the main parties, and most people think in terms of voting for that party or its leader rather than the individual candidate; they say 'I've always been Labour' or 'I'm voting for Boris'.

Anyone can stand for election

Whoever gets the most votes in each constituency is elected MP for that constituency. This system is called **first past the post**. Critics of first past the post point to its problems. One problem is that if the number of MPs in Parliament can be very different from the total number of votes cast for their party. For example, in the 2015 General Election, UKIP (the UK Independence Party) got nearly 4 million votes (12.6% of the votes cast) but only one MP (0.2% of the MPs) because their votes were spread across many constituencies. Another problem is that in certain areas, certain parties win almost all the time. This can make voters in those areas feel that there is not much point in voting as the result is always the same. Supporters of first past the post say that it gives a clear, simple result, and also that it gives everyone their own named MP to represent their area, to whom they can bring their local problems, whether they voted for him or her or not. They also say it is more likely to deliver an overall majority in parliament for one party, ensuring stable government (see below for an explanation of how this works). The alternative to first past the post is **proportional representation**, a system already used in many countries, whereby the number of MPs more nearly reflects the number of votes cast.

How are governments formed?

Once the election is over, we have 650 new MPs, who form the House of Commons. The Queen then appoints a Prime Minister and asks him or her to form a government.

Who gets to ride to Buck-ingham Palace for the job offer?

So who gets the ride in the bullet proof Jaguar to Buckingham Palace for the job offer? The leader of the party which can 'command the support' of the House of Commons. This means that their party can be sure of winning a vote in the House of Commons. To do that they will need the support of a majority of MPs. If one party has an **overall majority**, that is, they have more MPs than all the other parties combined, it is easy for the Queen to choose. For most of the twentieth century, elections were 'won' by just one party getting an overall majority. Recently, however, that has not always been the case. When no party has an overall majority, the result is known as a **hung parliament**. Most recently, the 2017 General Election created a hung parliament; the Conservatives were the largest party, but did not have an overall majority, so they had to do a deal with a small party from Northern Ireland, the Democratic Unionist Party (DUP) in order to form a government. In a hung parliament, small parties, and even individual MPs, have much more power, as they can get concessions from the government by threatening not to support them in a vote in parliament.

Who is the government?

The **government** is made up of **ministers**, each of whom has responsibility for a particular area, e.g. health, education, defence etc. They make decisions about how the health service, schools, the armed forces etc. are run. The head of the government is the **Prime Minister**. 'Prime' means first or most important. In theory, ministers are appointed by the Queen (they are called 'ministers of the crown'); in practice, they are appointed (and can be dismissed) by the Prime Minister. The leading ministers (about 20) form the **Cabinet**, chaired by the Prime Minister. The Cabinet makes decisions jointly about matters that affect the whole government. While they may debate these decisions vigorously in their meetings, once a decision is made, ministers are expected to support it. If they feel they cannot support it, they are expected to resign. Discussions in Cabinet meetings are supposed to be private, so that everyone can speak their mind freely.

How are laws passed?

For a new law to be passed, a bill to enact it it has to win a majority in a vote in the **House of Commons**. It then goes on to the **House of Lords**, which is made up mostly of quite a lot of people who have not been elected, but were chosen by leaders of the political parties, usually for long service. There are also a few members of the House of Lords who are hereditary, that is they only have the job because they inherited it from their fathers (never their mothers). The House of Lords debate all bills, and may make small changes to them, but in practice it is unusual for them to vote against the House of Commons. Their job (in theory) is to provide wise guidance and advice. Once a law has been passed by both the House of Commons and the House of Lords, the Queen signs the bill (this is called the Royal Assent) and it becomes law.

What about referendums?

Supporters of referendums say that they are much more directly democratic than parliamentary democracy. Critics say that they create division in a country because they reduce complicated issues to a simple, binary choice with no possibility of compromise or negotiation. In the 2016 referendum on the European Union, 52% voted Leave. This was presented by supporters of Brexit as proving that the 'will of the people' was that we should leave the EU. However, the fact is that unlike in some other countries (e.g. Switzerland), referendums have no official place in the British constitution.

Britain is a **parliamentary democracy**. This means that the will of the people is expressed not by referendums, still less by opinion polls, but by parliament, made up of MPs elected by the people. The 2016 referendum on EU membership was merely 'advisory', and had no force in law; that is, the government would have been quite entitled, under the British constitution, to say, 'Oh, so 52% of people want to leave the EU, do they? That's interesting. We still think on balance, though, that it would be better for the country to stay in the EU.' However, this would have been politically impossible.

Referendums have no official place in the British constitution

2 How the economy works

Economics is a school subject, but at present in the UK it is only studied in the sixth form, from age 16, and then only as an optional subject. I've never understood why it is not studied earlier. It is about how we organise society to allocate limited resources (both money and goods) in the fairest, most efficient and most effective way, and as such it touches on the most basic questions of values and how we think the world should be run (as you can see in the section on neo-liberalism vs social democracy in the last chapter).

The economy is the system by which goods and services are produced and exchanged

What is the economy?

The economy is the system by which goods and services are produced and exchanged. It isn't just people who run businesses or banks who participate in the economy. Every time you go to a shop or a café or a restaurant or buy something online, you are participating in the economy. If you have a job for which you are paid (even a paper round), you are participating in the economy. If you can't get a job; or if the job you have doesn't pay enough; or if you're still living with your parents because you can't afford to move out - that's an economic problem. The economy exists, whether we like it or not; without it we would have nowhere to live, nothing to wear, nothing to do and nothing to eat. So the economy is pretty fundamental.

Public sector and private sector

The economy is divided into the **public sector** and the **private sector**.

The **public sector** is the part of the economy which is owned and run by the government. In Britain, it includes:

- The National Health Service (the NHS)
- The road system
- The police
- The armed forces
- State (non fee-paying) schools
- Services provided by local councils, such as rubbish collection, libraries etc.

The **private sector** is everything else, owned either by private individuals or by public companies.

Public companies are, despite their name, not part of the public sector. They are so called because they are owned by shareholders. Shareholders are people who have bought shares in the company. Buying a share in a company means that you own a certain percentage of the company. If the company makes a profit (by receiving more in income for its goods or services than it spends on making or providing them), shareholders are paid a dividend, that is, a percentage of the profits based on how many shares they own.

Public company shares are bought and sold on the Stock Exchange. The value of the shares will go up and down depending on the demand for them, which is usually determined by how well the company is doing and is expected to do. As well as making money from dividends, you can make money by selling your shares at a higher price than you bought them.

Large companies are often international, with their UK holdings being only a small part of their worldwide operation. So, for example, when you buy a coffee from a café that is part of a global chain, you may be engaging with a business that is based in another country, and has thousands of outlets all round the world. Part of the money you pay for your coffee will go to shareholders in many different parts of the world. International businesses are harder for the government to control. Some companies may arrange their affairs so that they pay little or no tax in the UK, despite benefitting from many of the facilities provided by the public sector such as state education (ensuring their staff and customers can read the menu and count the change), the police (stopping people breaking into their cafés) and the roads (ensuring people can drive or take the bus to their cafés).

Social democrats tend to favour a larger public sector; neo-liberals tend to favour a larger private sector

Social democrats tend to favour a larger public sector; neo-liberals tend to favour a larger private sector. See Chapter 9 for the reasons for these beliefs.

The process of moving a business from the public sector to the private sector is called **privatisation**. Electricity, gas, water, the railways and telecommunications were once all in the public sector in the UK, until the Conservative government led by Margaret Thatcher in the 1980s privatised them. The process of moving a business from the private sector to the public sector is called **nationalisation**. Healthcare was in the private sector in the UK until 1948, when the creation of the NHS nationalised it.

Social democrats are more likely to favour nationalisation; neo-liberals tend to favour privatisation.

Tax

Tax is money raised by the government to pay for the public sector.

There are several different kinds of tax:

- **Income tax**. This is tax taken as a percentage of what you are paid.
- **Corporation tax**. This is tax on business profits.
- **Sales tax**. This is tax added to the price of goods or services you buy. In the UK, it is known as Value Added Tax, or VAT.
- **Council tax**. This is tax which helps pay for local services such as rubbish collection and libraries; it is paid by home owners, and it is based on the value of your property.

Currently, in the UK, income tax is **progressive taxation**; that is, the more you earn, the higher the percentage of your income you pay to the government. Some people argue for a **flat tax**, where everyone pays the same percentage. Some former communist countries, such as Russia and Latvia, already have a flat tax. Progressive taxation tends to make society a little more equal; flat taxation tends to maintain inequality.

Social democrats tend to be in favour of higher taxes; neo-liberals tend to be in favour of lower taxes. Simple arguments for / against tax are:

- The higher taxes are, the more the government has to spend on the things the public sector provides, and the better these are likely to be. A well funded public sector supports the private sector.
- The lower taxes are, the more money individuals and businesses have, and the more active and prosperous the economy will be. Also, low taxes tend to incentivise hard work.

Tax is money raised by the government to pay for the public sector

The Welfare State

The **welfare state** consists of benefits paid for by taxation and provided by the government to those who need them.

It includes:

- The NHS.
- Jobseeker's allowance, for people who do not have a job.
- Sickness and disability benefit, for people who are too ill / not able to work.
- Pensions, paid to everyone over the age of 65.
- Other benefits, such as free travel on buses for over 60s.

Neo-liberals tend to be in favour of reducing the welfare state; social democrats tend to be in favour of maintaining or expanding it.

Neo-liberals tend to be in favour of reducing the welfare state; social democrats tend to be in favour of maintaining or expanding it

What have we learnt in this chapter?

1. How Britain is run ☐
2. How the economy works ☐

Do this before you read the next chapter

Take some of the motions below. Prepare cases for and against them, using what you have learnt in this chapter, and doing some extra research to extend your knowledge.

How Britain is run

- This house would abolish the monarchy.
- This house would make voting in General Elections compulsory.
- This house would make it compulsory for 50% of MPs to be female.
- This house would introduce proportional representation.
- This house would abolish the House of Lords.
- This house would impose term limits on Prime Ministers.
- This house would make it compulsory for every other Prime Minister to be female.
- This house would ban referendums.

How the economy works

- This house would privatise the NHS.
- This house would nationalise the railways.
- This house would tax land.
- This house would introduce a flat tax.
- This house would introduce a maximum wage.
- This house would cut benefits.
- This house would boycott companies that do not pay tax in the UK.
- This house would introduce a carbon tax.

Tricks of the Trade

In this chapter, we'll be learning about rhetoric; how to use language to persuade.

'Rhetoric' is a Greek word, meaning *the art of persuasion*.

It's not surprising that rhetoric is a Greek word, as persuasive public speaking was big in Ancient Athens. Rhetoric is an important part of democracy, which the Ancient Athenians invented in or around 500 BC (democracy is also a Greek word - it means 'rule by the people'). Democracy involves, like debating, different ideas competing, supporters of each trying to persuade people to agree with them. Some people think that the Ancient Athenians sat around in the sunshine debating the issues of the day in a calm, rational manner, listening carefully to each other and nodding their heads appreciatively at a particularly well made point, pausing in their discussions only to chew an olive or sip some ouzo. It wasn't like that. Thousands of men (I'm afraid they were all men - and slaves weren't allowed either) would gather on a hill in Athens called the Pnyx for regular assemblies to discuss the business of the city. Supporters of different policies would put their point of view, but they had to fight to be heard. You had to be loud, confident, entertaining and wily to get people just to listen to you, never mind agree with you. And it wasn't only the assemblies; the courts were like that too. The Ancient Athenians were very litigious (that is, they liked suing each other a lot). But unlike in our system, juries did not consist of twelve people sitting quietly in a box listening to the evidence; they ran to the hundreds, and they didn't hold back in letting the litigants know what they thought of them.

So, rhetoric in Ancient Athens was big, and it became big business. There was a whole class of people known as sophists, who could make a very good living teaching citizens the tricks of rhetoric; how to use language to persuade. In this chapter, we're going to be learning some of these tricks. It's useful to know them, as using them in the right way will help make your speeches more persuasive. They all have Greek words to describe them, which you can drop in if you want to impress your English or Classics teacher, but I'll also give them descriptions in English for clarity.

Anaphora (varied repetition)

Repeating the same phrase at the beginning of several phrases, sentences or paragraphs. Probably the most famous example is Martin Luther King's speech in favour of equal rights for African Americans in Washington in 1963 in which he begins successive sentences with the phrase 'I have a dream … I have a dream …', fixing in his listeners' minds his vision of a better America. (It has become known as the 'I have a dream' speech.) In a speech on the motion, 'This house would make the use of homophobic language illegal' you might begin several sentences with 'Gay people walk in fear because …', each time giving a different example of homophobic violence.

Antithesis (balanced contrast)

Comparing one thing with another in balanced clauses. In debating, you would normally use this to compare what you are advocating with what your opponents are advocating, making it clear by the comparison that your version is better. For example, in the debate on making homophobic speech illegal, 'Do we want a world in which gay people walk in fear, or a world in which they walk in freedom?'

Argumentum ad populum (appeal to the people; actually a Latin phrase).

A direct appeal to the audience. A good way to make an emotional connection with your listeners. It can be in the form of a question ('Is there anyone in this room who would keep silent when they heard a gay person being abused?') or a statement ('I know that no one in this room would keep silent when they heard a gay person being abused.) Can be a high risk strategy if the audience is not on your side; they might not give you the answer you want.

Asyndeton (a list without conjunctions)

A good way to give the impression that the evidence is piling up on your side of the argument. 'Persecuted, reviled, insulted, humiliated, rejected; who can deny that gay people need the protection of this law?'

Chiasmus (balancing two inverted clauses)

A more sophisticated form of antithesis, in which you repeat a clause while reversing its terms, making it clear by the contrast, as in antithesis, that your version is better than your opponents'. Probably the most famous example is from President Kennedy's inauguration speech in 1961: 'Ask not what your country can do for you, but what you can do for your country.' To take our banning homophobic speech debate, you could say (for the opposition): 'Let us not seek to protect tolerance through the practice of intolerance; rather, let us fight intolerance through the practice of tolerance.'

Dialysis (setting out two equally unacceptable alternatives)

This device seeks to show that whatever follows from your opponent's proposal, it will not be good, by giving two possible outcomes, both of which are bad. For example: 'If we make homophobic speech illegal, either homophobes will continue to abuse gay people openly, presenting themselves as martyrs for free speech, or they will do so anonymously on social media, with even greater venom; either way, homophobia will thrive.'

Enargia (painting a picture)

This is when you describe a place or situation, either imagined or real, so vividly that the audience can see it. It can be very emotionally powerful. 'Harry comes home, goes up to his bedroom, and switches on his phone. On it are forty-seven messages, each one insulting him for being gay. He looks out of the window. He can see his brother playing football in the garden with a gang of other boys. He can hear his sister in the next room laughing on the phone to her best friend. They have friends, they are happy, but everyone hates Harry, because he is gay. Tears come into his eyes. He picks up his old, battered teddy bear, whose ear is nearly falling off, and clutches it to him for comfort. The phone beeps. He knows it will be another abusive message, but still he reaches for the phone, his hand shaking ...'

Epiplexis (a series of rhetorical questions)

This is when you ask several rhetorical questions (see **erotema** below), usually to express anger or indignation. 'Are we going to stand by as gay teenagers are bullied? Will we do nothing as they self-harm? Will we remain silent as the suicide rate mounts? Will we be able to sleep at night if we do nothing? Are we really that unfeeling?'

Epistrophe (repeated endings)

This is a kind of opposite version of **anaphora**, in which the same word or phrase is repeated at the end of phrases or sentences. 'Controlling what people write in newspapers is oppressive; saying what they can't write online is oppressive; monitoring what they message or say on phones is oppressive; censoring what they say to each other is oppressive; intervening, perhaps, even in what they think, is nothing but oppressive.'

Erotema (rhetorical question)

A question which doesn't expect or need an answer. 'Is it right that gay teenagers should walk in fear?' 'Do we want to live in a society where you can be sent to prison for what you say?'

Hypophora (asking yourself questions and answering them)

This is a technique much used by politicians, as it makes it look as if they are subjecting themselves to scrutiny, when in fact it is the equivalent of setting your own exam and then marking it yourself. However, it can be an effective, easy to follow way of setting out a case. 'Why should we make homophobic speech illegal? Because words are not just words; they lead to actions. How do they lead to actions? Abusive language licenses violence. How does it license violence? If you demean people in the way you speak about them, you make it more acceptable to attack them physically.'

Metanoia (saying something then retracting it)

You can use this to ramp up your condemnation of something you want to criticise, or increase your praise for something you want to celebrate, by finding ever more extreme terms. 'Making homophobic language illegal is unfair. No, not unfair - it is absurd. No, more than absurd - it is tyrannical!'

Metaphor (comparing something to something else)

Metaphor includes simile. It is one of the first things you learn in English lessons from a very early age, and is much deployed in creative writing, so you should be familiar with it. You can use it very effectively in speeches too, to make your arguments more vivid. 'Making certain words illegal is like making us walk around with a policeman sitting on our shoulder.'

Paralipsis (saying something that you say you're not going to say)

This is when you say something while apparently denying you're saying it. It makes it look as if you can't say it because it is so shocking, and so adds to its power. 'I'm not going to go into the consequences of homophobic bullying. The isolation of its victims. The despair. The depression. The anxiety. The self-harm. The suicide attempts. That's not what we're here to discuss. We're here, according to the opposition, to discuss free speech ...'

Polysyndeton (a list with conjunctions)

This has a similar effect to **asyndeton** of piling on examples relentlessly. The only difference is that it uses conjunctions such as 'and'. 'Hatred and bigotry and contempt and disgust and rejection; this is what gay people face every day.'

Symploce (beginning and ending sentences with the same words or phrases)

This is a kind of mash-up of **anaphora** and **epistrophe** for added repetitive effect. 'Homophobic language is offensive, but it's still legal. Homophobic language demeans people for who they are, but it's still legal. Homophobic language threatens people for who they are, but it's still legal. Homophobic language causes violence; it's still legal.'

Tricolon (list of three)

The most famous example in literature of **tricolon** is in the opening of Mark Anthony's funeral speech for Caesar in Shakespeare's *Julius Caesar*: 'Friends, Romans, countrymen ...'. Another example, this time from history, is the real Julius Caesar's comment on a military victory: 'I came, I saw, I conquered.' Both build up to a kind of mini-climax, and this is what makes this device effective. 'Making the use of homophobic language illegal would be unreasonable, oppressive and tyrannical.' 'Making the use of homophobic language illegal is just, effective and an urgent necessity.'

What have we learnt in this chapter?

1. How to identify and describe some common rhetorical devices ☐
2. What makes them effective ☐

Do this before you read the next chapter

- Watch or listen to some classic political speeches online (e.g. Lincoln's Gettysburg Address; Mark Anthony's funeral speech in Shakespeare's *Julius Caesar*; Churchill's 'We shall fight them on the beaches …' speech; Martin Luther King's 'I have a dream' speech; Barack Obama's speech on the night he was elected in 2008) and see how many of these devices you can spot.

- In pairs in your debating club, give speeches to each other using as many of these devices as possible. See how many the person listening can spot and list.

CHAPTER 12

Motions That Matter

In this chapter, we're going to be learning about how to devise successful motions, and about how different kinds of motions work in different kinds of debates.

It's easy for a debater to feel passive about motions. They're just what you get given; you have to get on with proposing or opposing them, whether you like it or not.

It's important, though, for a debater to think actively about motions. You should think about how motions are constructed; what different types of motion demand from debaters; and what challenges and opportunities different motions present.

A successful motion must be balanced

Drawing up your own list of motions is a very worthwhile exercise. A good stock of motions is an invaluable resource for a school debating club, providing material for practice in training sessions, and also for use in any internal competitions you run. The more motions you have, the more you understand how motions work, and also the more you understand how to analyse motions when you are preparing for a debate.

So, in this chapter we're going to be learning about:

- What makes a successful motion.
- What the different types of motion are.

What makes a successful motion?

- A successful motion must be **balanced**. That is, it must be possible to make more or less equally strong arguments on both sides of the case, without stretching either evidence, reality or morality to unacceptable limits for either side.

  'This house believes that climate change is a problem' stretches the use of **evidence** to unacceptable limits for the opposition.

  'This house would make the use of jet-packs compulsory for all journeys within cities' stretches **reality** to unacceptable limits for the proposition.

  'This house would introduce compulsory euthanasia for disabled people' stretches **morality** to unacceptable limits for the proposition.

- A successful motion must be **narrow** enough in scope to be discussed within a five minute speech, but also **broad** enough in scope to sustain a full debate.

  'This house would do more to stop climate change' is too **broad**.

'This house would stop Year 10s buying water in plastic bottles from the corner shop on the way to school when they could bring in their own bottles and fill them up from the water fountain outside the gym instead' is too **narrow**, however well intentioned.

- A successful motion must be **appropriate** to the cultural, academic and age context of the debaters it is allocated to.

  'This house would respond to an economic recession by deploying a Keynesian model of deficit spending' is probably not the ideal motion for the first session of the Year Seven debating club, though it could be a great exercise in an A-Level Economics class (see Chapter 13, How To Use Debating in Lessons).

  'This house thinks dogs make better pets than cats' might come across as seriously patronising if used in the final of a sixth form debating competition, but is ideal for introducing Years Five and Six to debating.

  'This house would introduce stricter gun control laws' will spark lively and impassioned discussions in the US, but doesn't make much sense in the UK, where gun control laws are already very strict.

  'This house would abolish Christmas' is a great one for a fun debate at the end of term in December in a church school, but doesn't work so well in a Muslim school in May.

Be sensitive also to the way in which debate topics which may touch on personal issues for students. 'This house believes that the fashion and beauty industry helps cause eating disorders' is not the best choice if you have a student in the debating club who has, or is recovering from, an eating disorder. 'This house would introduce automatic prison sentences for anyone carrying a knife' might be best postponed if you have a student in the club close to someone who has recently been a victim of knife crime.

Make your motions appropriate

What different types of motion are there?

Policy motions are easier

Policy vs principle

The most basic distinction (about which we learnt in Chapter 2, How Debating Works) is between **policy** motions and **ideas** motions; that is, you remember, motions which begin 'This house would ...' and motions which begin 'This house believes ...'

In general, **policy** motions are easier to tackle, and are therefore more appropriate for novices, because it is easier to focus on specific and concrete measures. Ideas motions are harder to define and pin down, so are more challenging, but can also lead to very interesting discussions.

So, 'This house would ban mobile phones from schools' is very specific and concrete, and therefore relatively straightforward.

'This house believes money does not bring happiness' is much more vague and general, and needs very careful definition to pin it down, while at the same time opening up really big and fascinating questions about the true nature of happiness.

Familiar vs unfamiliar

Familiar motions deal with issues all students have direct experience of, usually to do with school. They're great for novice debaters.

Classic **familiar** motions are:

- This house would make all schools co-educational.
- This house would abolish school uniform.
- This house would abolish homework.
- This house would make school voluntary.
- This house would abolish exams.

Unfamiliar motions deal with issues beyond students' experience, and may require very specific knowledge to make sense of them. Students debating these motions have to extend themselves by doing some research / using their general knowledge. (For some of this useful general knowledge, see Chapter 10, What Debaters Need to Know About the World; for advice on research / how to extend your general knowledge, see Chapter 15, Onwards ...). These motions can work particularly well for long prep debates, or within the curriculum as part of subject-specific study (see Chapter 13, How Debating Can Be Used in Lessons).

Examples of **unfamiliar** motions are:

- This house would introduce proportional representation in UK General Elections.
- This house believes nuclear power is the answer to our energy needs.
- This house would introduce term limits for Prime Ministers.
- This house would ban genetically modified food.
- This house believes globalisation is a force for good.

The most exciting debates arise in response to unfore-seeable events

Topical motions

Some of the most exciting and compelling debates can arise in response to very immediate, unforeseeable events and issues. I vividly remember, early in my debating career, running a debate shortly after the terrorist attacks in America on September 11th, 2001, commonly referred to as '9/11'. The school I teach in has a large number of students with American connections, and the school community was still reeling in shock from what had happened, trying to make sense of it (as was the whole world). I set the motion 'This house supports the invasion of Afghanistan'. Normally, I was doing well if the numbers in the audience got into double figures. That day, there were over a hundred students crammed into the room. As much as anything else, that debate was a cathartic experience, allowing students to speak and think about an issue that had affected them very deeply. The debate I staged on the Brexit referendum in 2016 (see Chapter 1, Why Do

Debating?) had a similar impact, as have more informal, but very well attended, discussions on the issues raised by the #MeToo movement, school shootings in the US and climate change.

I also recommend staging debates as part of mock elections to coincide with General Elections. You can stage these in whole school assembly, with one speaker for each of the main parties (with instructions to focus on issues rather than personalities), followed by an immediate opportunity for everyone present to vote in a secret ballot. The results of this vote can be very revealing, and are often surprising! This is an example of how debating can perform a public, civic function, by engaging all students actively in politics.

Be sensitive, of course, when staging these very public debates to what it is appropriate to discuss in a school. If in doubt, consult senior leadership.

What is topical changes

Obviously, what is topical changes. 'This house would ban smoking in public places' and 'This house would legalise same-sex marriage' were once hot topics, but now that smoke-free pubs and gay weddings are firmly established in both the law and the culture of Britain, these motions no longer make sense. Part of being a successful debater (and a successful debating coach) is having finely tuned antennae for what the big issues of the moment are, and how they can be approached.

One last word about motions. There is not an infinite number of them. If (as I hope you will) you have a long career in debating, it is likely that you will come across the same motion more than once. If this does happen, do not think 'Great! I won that debate last time, so I can reuse my preparation.' Approach each motion as if for the first time. This is partly because it will make your performance fresher; partly because your opponents this time will not be the same as your opponents last time; and partly because, even if you won last time, you should have learnt something from the judge's feedback on that occasion, and should be adapting your approach in response to that feedback.

What have we learnt in this chapter?

1. What makes a successful motion ☐
2. What different kinds of motion there are ☐
3. Which motions are appropriate for which debaters ☐

Do this before you read the next chapter

- In your debating club, draw up a list of possible motions.
- Discuss which motions are appropriate for which debates / debaters.
- Practise preparing different motions.
- Set up a central database of possible motions that everyone in the club can access.

CHAPTER 13

How to use debating in lessons

In this chapter, we're going to learn how debating can be used in the curriculum.

This chapter is mostly directed at teachers, as it tells them how they can use debating in their lessons. However, students can read it too. They can use the persuasive techniques they have learnt in debating to convince their teachers they should have more debates in lessons. Make it clear to your teachers that they don't have to be a 'debating teacher' to do this.

In one sense, all teachers do debating. It's a fundamental part of what happens in every classroom. Every time a teacher asks a question which could have more than one answer you are beginning to debate. There is a perception that debate is the domain of humanities subjects: is Shylock a victim or a villain? (English); was Elizabeth 1 a good or a bad queen? (History); is euthanasia ever justified? (Philosophy). But there is a place for it in all subjects. Should patent law apply to medical drugs? (Chemistry); should zoos be banned? (Biology); is nuclear power the answer to our energy needs? (Physics); should the government make decisions based on statistical evidence? (Maths). Thinking through different options, weighing up pros and cons, is what we get our students to do all the time. What debating does is give a formal structure to this process, forcing students to collect evidence, analyse that evidence, structure arguments, and respond to challenges to those arguments; all skills which, it's easy to see, are eminently transferable to any subject.

So: how do you set one up in your classroom?

Every time a teacher asks a question which could have more than one answer you are beginning to debate

Choosing the motion

Looking back at the topics we started with, what does a good motion for a lesson look like?

This house believes that Shakespeare presents Shylock as a sympathetic character. (English: challenging, because broad.)

This house would not prosecute Shylock for his attempted assault on Antonio. (English: easier, because more specific.)

This house believes Elizabeth 1 was a good queen. (History; challenging because so broad.)

This house would not have outlawed the Catholic Mass in Elizabethan England. (History: easier, because more specific, though also needing more specific knowledge.)

This house would legalise assisted dying. (Philosophy: a good combination of theoretical - is euthanasia moral? - and practical - under what circumstances should it be legal?)

What does a good motion for a lesson look like?

This house would limit patents on medical drugs to five years. (Chemistry / Economics: helpfully specific, though requiring knowledge about patent laws and how they work. At the same time, it deals with big questions about freedom from vs freedom to. See Chapter 9, The Big Issues, for further discussion of this dichotomy.)

This house would ban nuclear energy. (Physics: helpfully specific and concrete, but also requiring a lot of specific knowledge.)

This house would ban zoos. (Biology: also helpfully specific, but will work much better if students are encouraged to research specifics on animal welfare rather than rely on naive anthropomorphic arguments about how cute bears are and you wouldn't like it if someone could look into your bedroom 24 /7.)

This house would allow people to vote for as many candidates as they like in General Elections. (Maths: very specific, but with a basis in subject knowledge. Apparently there is a mathematical reason why this system might be fairer, but I'm not good enough at Maths to understand it. I'd like to hear the debate to find out.)

How to run the lesson

The obvious problem is that a maximum of eight people can be involved in a debate (see Chapter 2, How Debating Works), and most classes have more than eight students.

There are various ways round this:

- Divide the class into groups and have them all prepare a debate, and then pick, either at random or by differentiation, one or two groups to give 'show debates'. The rest of the class can still join in by making points from the floor. This keeps the class focused, and can be a good way to use the debate as a teaching tool; you can refer to the points raised in your plenary.
- (If you have a lot of time, e.g. at the end of term) as above, only stagger the debates over several lessons. You can add a little spice to this by making it competitive, awarding a prize to the best debaters at the end.

- Run several debates simultaneously, enforcing time limits centrally. This obviously makes for a very noisy classroom (it helps if it is also a big classroom) but it does have the advantage that everyone gets a go, and it also makes it easier for students who find public performance difficult.
- You can run a variation on the simultaneous debate format by setting up more or less spontaneous mini-debates in pairs ('We've been discussing whether Shakespeare makes Shylock sympathetic or not. Discuss this in pairs: first person says why he's sympathetic for three minutes; second person says why he isn't'.) These can be dropped into a lesson at short notice with very little preparation.

For all except the last example, you need to set up the desks so that students on different sides are facing each other.

Why use debate in the classroom?

It teaches:

- Research skills
- Team work
- How to speak confidently in public
- How to use evidence well
- How to build arguments
- How to analyse arguments
- An empathetic understanding of different points of view
- How democracy works

It also helps you to meet your statutory requirement to promote the British values of democracy and mutual respect for those of different faiths and beliefs, and is an excellent way of furthering spiritual, moral, social and cultural education.

So, the value of using debating in the classroom is, er .... beyond debate.

So, the value of using debating in the classroom is, er ... beyond debate

CHAPTER 14

Masterclass

In this chapter, we'll be listening in on a high quality debate, analysing what the debaters do well, and thinking about how they could do even better.

One of the best ways to learn how to do something is to observe an expert doing it. This applies very much to debating. Watch as many debates as you can, either live or online. Watch them as a judge would watch (see Chapter 8), analysing what the debaters are doing well, and what they could do better.

Debates (especially good ones) are often fast and furious, and it can be hard to keep up with them. That's one advantage of watching them on video, where you can pause the film to reflect and make notes, much as a sports coach might analyse a game. It's rare, though, to have a full transcript of a debate. This chapter gives you a transcript. The debate never actually happened - it is a work of fiction - but it is based on the many debates I have watched and judged over the years. I've chosen to use British Parliamentary (BP) format, as I think it is slightly more demanding than Mace, and gives more opportunity to exemplify the key debating skills. See Chapter 2, How Debating Works, to remind yourself of how BP works. All the debaters are experienced and skilled, though they are not perfect, and do make mistakes. I give a running commentary on the debate in my notes. At the end, the judge gives a rank order; see if, as you read the debate, you can work out what the rank order should be.

Motion: This house would make it compulsory for 50% of MPs to be female

(This type of motion is often known as a 'quotas' motion, and is a common topic. It could be about employment or educational background or, as here, political representation, and the quotas might apply to race, educational background, class, sexuality, or, as here, gender.)

CHAIR

Welcome everyone to this debate. To remind you of the rules; each speaker will have five minutes to speak, with the first and last minute protected. I will signal the beginning and end of protected time by banging once on the table like this. (*Bang.*) At the end of the five minutes, I will signal that time is up by banging twice on the table like this (*Two bangs.*) Speakers will then have fifteen seconds to finish their speeches; if they are still speaking after fifteen seconds, I will bang on the table continuously like this (*continuous bangs*) and the speaker must sit down immediately. As this is BP, there will be no speeches from the floor. At the end of the debate, the judge will give her feedback and the result.[1]

The motion before the house is: '**This house would make it compulsory for 50% of MPs to be female.**' I'd like now to ask the Prime Minister to open the debate.

PRIME MINISTER

Thank you, Madam Chair.

Britain is a representative democracy. MPs are elected by the British people, to represent the British people. And yet, MPs don't look like the British people.[2]

Why not?[3]

Because, as you may have noticed, 50% of the British people are female; one in every two[4]. And yet, following the 2019 General Election, only 34%[5] - barely more than one in three - of MPs are female. So, our representative democracy is not doing its job; to represent.[6]

This has to change. Only when the composition of Parliament fairly represents the composition of the nation will we be fairly governed.[7]

We therefore propose that it should be compulsory for 50% of MPs to be female. We will achieve this goal in the following way. The current 650 constituencies[8] will be reduced to 325, with each new, larger constituency electing two MPs, one

1 It's usually a good idea to run quickly through the rules if you are Chair, just to remind everyone, and make sure everyone knows what they have to do.

2 Notice how the Prime Minister is using epistrophe (repeated endings) (see Chapter 11). By focusing attention through repetition on the phrase 'the British people', she appeals to her audience by directly addressing them and including them; as this debate takes place in Britain, she can assume almost all the audience will be part of 'the British people'. Mark Antony uses a similar technique with his opening phrase 'Friends, Romans, countrymen' in Shakespeare's ***Julius Caesar.***

3 Now she's using hypophora (asking herself a question and answering it) (see Chapter 11). This is a good way to present her main argument to the audience in a clear, systematic way.

4 Most people know that 50% means one in two, but expressing the statistic in a different way further emphasises its significance when compared with the upcoming statistic about the percentage of women MPs.

5 This is obviously a crucial fact to know in this debate. Given that BP is short prep with no access to the internet, the Prime Minister must have known it already. Having some of these sorts of facts and figures at your fingertips will give you a great advantage.

6 The Prime Minister has started by saying what's wrong with 'Now' (see Chapter 5).

7 Here she introduces the 'Then' (see Chapter 5).

8 Another useful fact the Prime Minister has made sure she knows.

from a male list, one from a female list. This will retain the connection between MPs and their constituents and allow each party to put up both male and female candidates in every constituency, while ensuring completely equal access to Parliament for both men and women.[9]

(CHAIR gives the one minute knock)[10]

I will be explaining how this measure will ensure that women will be more likely to enter politics; how it will change the culture of politics; and how it will ensure that women's interests are considered when laws are made.[11] The Deputy Prime Minister[12] will show how this measure will change the way women are perceived in wider society; how it will inspire young women to achieve as highly, or more highly, than men; and how it will ultimately lead to a more civilised society.[13]

To my first point. Women are currently discouraged from entering politics because they are outnumbered in Parliament.

OPPOSITION WHIP[14]

On a point of information.

PRIME MINISTER

Yes please.[15]

OPPOSITION WHIP

The percentage of MPs who are female has steadily increased over recent years; there is no reason to suppose it should not continue to do so.[16]

PRIME MINISTER

That is the case, and it is very welcome.[17] I can see that my opponent clearly shares our desire for women to achieve equal representation[18] in Parliament; but only our measure will guarantee this.[19]

To return to my first point. Imagine an idealistic young woman who wants to change the world

9 This is 'the mechanism' (see Chapter 3, The Basic Skills), essential in a debate proposing a change to the status quo. It shows how the proposition will get from 'Now' to 'Then'. It is specific and practical, and also makes sure to anticipate possible objections, by conceding the importance of MPs representing their constituencies and of parties being allowed to select both male and female candidates. However, it is not beyond criticism, as we shall see.

10 Signposting of key points all done in the first minute; now time to move on to the substance.

11 Excellent signposting; three points (the right number), clearly and concisely stated, all showing what 'Then' would look like. Not much yet on why 'Then' will be better than 'Now'.

12 It feels a bit pompous at first to use these terms when you're used to calling your debating partner just 'Ben', but it helps you to get into the role.

13 The second half of the signposting shows that the two of them are working as a team, dividing up the points clearly between them. The fact that the Prime Minister focuses on politics, and the Deputy Prime Minister on wider society, makes the division even clearer and easier to understand.

14 Remember in BP anyone from any position on the other side of the table can make a POI.

15 A good time for the Prime Minister to take a point of information (POI), with her first point introduced.

16 The Opposition Whip is using line of attack #13 from Chapter 6, 'The problem will go away without the solution you propose'. It has some impact as it is based on a measurable fact (again, see how useful general knowledge about politics is for debaters), and it does diminish the severity of the problem in 'Then'; if the number of female MPs were dropping, the proposition would have a much more powerful case. The POI is also admirably concise and focused. It would be even better, though, if it was addressed to what the Prime Minister is saying at that moment.

17 Always agree with your opponent as much as you can without conceding your case; it is a very good way of disarming them.

18 'equal representation' is an astute choice of language, very helpful for the proposition in a 'quotas' debate. It makes it sound as if your measure is fair for the whole population, rather than just meeting the needs of one part of it. Compare the way in which the terms 'gay marriage' or 'same-sex marriage' imply something that meets only the needs of the gay community, while 'equal marriage' is more inclusive, implying that the measure treats everyone, straight and gay alike, the same.

Choice of language influences how people think about issues; to give another example, supporters of legal abortion describe themselves as 'pro-choice', not 'pro-abortion' (not everyone likes abortion, but everyone likes choice, as it gives them control over their lives), while opponents of abortion describe themselves as 'pro-life' (not everyone is opposed to abortion, but who could be opposed to life?). One of the ways in which the opening speaker in a debate can take control of it is by choosing the language in which the debate is conducted to benefit their side.

19 This is brilliant. The Prime Minister has caught the Opposition Whip out conceding her central point that equal representation is necessary, and shown that a/ they both want the same thing b/ her measure is more certain to achieve it. All while appearing friendly and nice by agreeing with him!

for the better. She watches debates in Parliament; they are dominated by men. She joins the local branch of her chosen party; it is dominated by men. She makes it on to a shortlist of candidates to stand for Parliament; this, too, is dominated by men. None the less, she is selected, and goes on to be elected an MP. On her first day, full of idealistic fervour, she walks into the chamber of the House of Commons ... to see the green benches covered by overwhelmingly male bottoms.[20] How many women would give up - do give up - before they even get this far?[21]

Imagine, now, a world where it was guaranteed by law that 50% of MPs would be women, and that every citizen would be represented by both a male MP and a female MP. A world where female participation in politics was taken for granted. A world where it would not so much as enter a young woman's head that she should not enter politics because of her gender.[22]

So, our measure would have a significant benefit in encouraging and empowering women to enter politics.

I will now go on to show how greater female participation in politics will benefit us all.[23]

Parliament currently resembles nothing so much as a boys' public school. The outdated Victorian architecture, setting one side against the other; the unfamily-friendly working hours, starting late and regularly going on till 10 or 11 at night; the jeering and baying that goes on at Prime Minister's Questions, like an out of control class. This toxic atmosphere must surely impact the quality of decision making.[24] Imagine, though, if it turned from being a boys' school that has reluctantly accepted a few girls into a fully co-educational school, with equal numbers of women. Women's tendency to work in a collaborative, consensual way and their desire for a better work-life balance could transform the culture of Parliament and thereby the quality of decision making.[25]

DEPUTY LEADER OF THE OPPOSITION

On a point of information.[26]

PRIME MINISTER

Yes please.

DEPUTY LEADER OF THE OPPOSITION

Isn't it an absurd generalisation to assume that women are never confrontational, and that men are incapable of being collaborative?[27] Aren't there, in any case, many situations in which

20 Here the Prime Minister is using enargia, painting an imaginary picture, showing us 'Now' and what is wrong with it. This has the advantage of making her point more vivid, while avoiding logical fallacy #3 (see Chapter 7), argument by anecdote, because it refers to a generic 'young woman', rather than one individual. She is also using (again) epistrophe, with her repetition of 'dominated by men'. The mention of 'bottoms' at the end might get a snigger or two. Humour can be an effective way of disarming your opponents. It's harder to disagree with someone when they're making you laugh.

21 Erotema (rhetorical question), doing the job of reminding us of one of the things that's wrong with 'Now'. Also metanoia - interrupting yourself with a qualification to show that things are even worse than you first thought.

22 Anaphora, repeating 'a world where ...' fixing this notion of a better future in our mind. Also, enargia, this time painting a picture of a better 'Then'.

23 After the rhetorical flourishes of her story of the idealistic young woman, the Prime Minister now sums up her first point crisply and clearly, and links neatly to her next point.

24 Setting up the 'Now' of parliamentary culture and what's wrong with it. However, the 'must surely' reveals a certain insecurity about the link between current parliamentary practices and the quality of decision making; she hasn't proved that this culture inevitably leads to bad decision making. Nor has she given any examples of bad decision making.

25 Now she gives us the 'Then' of how things would be different in her proposed future. Again, though, she doesn't do much to show the link between 50% female MPs and improved decision making.

26 A good time for the Deputy Leader of the Opposition to pounce, as the Prime Minister has deployed weak arguments

27 This is a model POI, as it identifies very crisply and concisely the weakness in the argument; both the 'Now' and the 'Then' are unconvincing scenarios, as they assume too much without satisfactory proof. Phrasing it as a rhetorical question puts responsibility for dealing with the issue back to the Prime Minister.

injustice, incompetence or even just inefficiency[28] demand a confrontational approach?[29]

PRIME MINISTER

Of course women can and should be confrontational on occasion.[30] My point is rather that the reset of parliament provided by the introduction of equal representation would greatly improve its culture.[31]

(CHAIR knocks for four minutes)

Now to the way in which equal representation would ensure justice for women.[32] The tampon tax; period poverty; inadequate provision for maternity leave; the gender pay gap; sexual harassment; domestic violence; the appallingly low rates of conviction for rape.[33] These are all injustices[34] which affect women exclusively, and all injustices which changes in the law could address. Isn't the fact that so many of these injustices are still unaddressed at least in part because of the inequality of representation in Parliament? Wouldn't these injustices, blighting the lives of millions of women, be better addressed by an equal Parliament?[35]

So, I have shown you that our current situation of unequal representation deters women from entering politics, creates a toxic culture in Parliament, and leaves injustices affecting women unaddressed.[36] Our proposal, ensuring equal representation for women in Parliament while maintaining the right of both constituency parties and voters to select their own candidates and their own MPs, will make Parliament both fairer and more effective, and will also make women's lives better.[37]

(CHAIR knocks for five minutes)[38]

28 A reversed tricolon (see Chapter 11). Normally tricolons are crescendos, building up to a climax. This one, however, is a diminuendo, starting with the solemn accusation of 'injustice' and going down to the less serious 'inefficiency'. This is a way of showing that the confrontational approach has value in both great and small situations, and therefore has universal scope.

29 Hitting your opponent with two different objections is the equivalent of following up a jab with a hook in boxing. The first weakens her; the second might floor her.

30 The Prime Minister has been forced to concede the Deputy Leader of the Opposition's point. Sometimes you have to accept a small defeat when confronted with a point you can't deny; although conceding an opponent's point may be a setback, to deny the strength of the point in the teeth of the evidence would look worse.

31 There's no doubt that the Deputy Leader of the Opposition won this particular exchange. The rather vague term 'reset' does not provide a clear route to 'Then', and the no less vague 'greatly improve its culture', similarly does not provide a clear picture of an improved 'Then'.

32 The Prime Minister recovers herself, and crisply introduces her third point.

33 This is a very powerful sentence. It uses asyndeton (see Chapter 11) to great effect, accumulating examples of injustice that women suffer, and builds to a crescendo, moving from economic inequalities suffered by women (maternity leave, tax on tampons) up to assaults on their physical safety (domestic violence, rape).

34 Language choice again. A weaker speaker might have used the word 'issues', which suggests something neutral, while 'injustices' describes something that is clearly wrong.

35 Erotema again; two rhetorical questions, using the doubling 'jab / hook' move; if you don't accept the first one, you might at least accept the second one.

36 Good signposting (see Chapter 3), summing up her arguments crisply in one sentence.

37 A crescendo tricolon to finish. Good to end on 'women's lives'. What happens in Parliament can (even though MPs make laws which affect all of us) seem a bit niche; but 'women's lives' encompasses 50% of the population.

38 In terms of timing, signposting and structure, the Prime Minister's speech is exemplary. It's less certain when it comes to argumentation. Her first and third arguments are strong, but her second is weak and underdeveloped, and quickly picked off by an effective POI. She wins one POI and loses the other.

It's early to say who is ahead at this stage (when we haven't yet heard any of the other side's speeches); however, I'd say that two out of three strong arguments and a strong response to the first POI from the Opposition Whip for the Prime Minister balanced against a weak second argument demolished by a devastating POI from the Deputy Leader of the Opposition makes it about 50 / 50 between Proposition and Opposition. Remember, though, that the contest in BP is not between Proposition and Opposition but between the four different teams. The judge will be noting how POIs are used as well as how speeches are given; the Leader of the Opposition / Deputy Leader of the Opposition team are ahead of the Member of the Opposition / Opposition Whip team on this measure.

CHAIR

May I thank the Prime Minister for her fine speech,[39] and invite the Leader of the Opposition to give his reply.

LEADER OF THE OPPOSITION

Thank you, Madam Chair.

The plan proposed by the Government side[40] is undemocratic, unnecessary and counter-productive.[41] It is undemocratic because it denies choice to voters; it is unnecessary because the problems it is trying to address can be better dealt with in other ways; it is counter-productive because it will actually make the problems it is trying to address worse.[42]

I will be showing how the proposed measure undermines the principle that voters can choose their own MPs; how the aim of encouraging greater participation by women in politics can be better achieved otherwise; and how the proposed measure will actually diminish the respect in which women in politics are held. The Deputy Leader of the Opposition will point to the dangers of 'mega-constituencies',[43] to the sexism implicit in the Government's proposal, and to its inadequacy as a measure for tackling inequality and prejudice.[44]

First, though, to some rebuttal.[45]

The Prime Minister claims firstly that women are discouraged from entering politics because of its domination by men. That might come as news to Arlene Foster, Nicola Sturgeon and Theresa May, who have recently been, or still are, the leaders of the Northern Irish, Scottish and British governments respectively.[46]

(CHAIR knocks for one minute)

It is an assertion that would also have been met with bafflement by Margaret Thatcher, who was not discouraged, at a time when the number of women MPs was far lower[47], from becoming our first woman Prime Minister in 1979. It is, moreover, seriously patronising and not a little sexist; is she suggesting that women are incapable of making

39 Don't let this praise go to your head. It's traditional for the Chair to praise all the speeches, just as a matter of courtesy. It would be quite inappropriate, though, for the Chair to give any kind of feedback on any speeches or suggest that one is better than another; that is the job of the Judge.

40 It's conventional in BP to refer to the Proposition as 'the Government', and the Opposition as 'the Opposition'.

41 Fine use of tricolon, also nicely signposting the Leader of the Opposition's case.

42 Expanding on the tricolon, amplifying the headline words. Gradually expanding your case is a very effective way of introducing it and fixing it in your audience's mind.

43 This shows that the Leader / Deputy Leader of the Opposition have been working and thinking fast, listening carefully to the Prime Minister's speech, perhaps passing notes to each other (talking during someone else's speech is not allowed). They are responding rapidly to the mechanism proposed by the Prime Minister. Alternatively, they may have anticipated this as a possible mechanism and planned for it during their prep time.

Also note the clever use of language in 'mega-constituencies'. Just as the Prime Minister's use of 'equal representation' made her measure look natural and fair, this neologism (invented word) makes the proposed larger constituencies sound overwhelming and scary.

(Here is a good example of how changing the language can change the debate. In the late 1980s, Margaret Thatcher's Conservative government decided they wanted to change the system of local taxation from one where only home owners paid tax to one where everyone who lived in an area paid tax to run its services. They called this the 'community charge'. 'Community' sounds friendly and collaborative, implying everyone has a stake in the area; 'charge' suggests money paid for something in return. Their opponents, though, started calling it the 'poll tax'. 'Poll' implied you wouldn't be allowed to vote if you didn't pay it, and therefore as if democracy had gone from being a right to something you had to pay for; 'tax' sounded like 'taxing', implying something unpleasant and burdensome. The name 'poll tax' stuck, and did much to turn people against the measure. The poll tax's unpopularity played a large part in Margaret Thatcher being overthrown as Prime Minister in 1990; her successor, John Major, scrapped the tax soon after. Words matter!)

44 As with the Prime Minister, the job of the Leader of the Opposition is to signpost not only his arguments but his partner's.

45 Rebuttal is essential in every speech bar the first one.

46 Another handy snippet of political general knowledge. Keep a notebook to write this sort of thing down in; you never know when it might come in handy. As hard copy resources (unlike internet research) are allowed in short prep debates, you can take your notebook with you to debates.

47 You would, however, have to be a seriously hardcore political nerd to know the number of women MPs in 1979 (it's 19 [3%]; I looked it up), so 'far lower' is near enough to make the point and vague enough to be not inaccurate.

their own way in politics without having all obstacles removed for them?[48]

Second,[49] she claims that women are somehow nicer people, more collaborative and less confrontational, and that this will lead to better decision making. This is, once again, patronising and sexist, attributing particular qualities to particular genders.[50] Moreover, the very confrontationalism she criticises can be a great strength, and one deployed to great effect by women; Margaret Thatcher[51] became one of the most dynamic and effective Prime Ministers in our history precisely because she was not afraid to confront her opponents.

Thirdly, she claims that only a 50% female Parliament can deal with issues that concern women. This is a very dangerous argument, that only people affected by issues can satisfactorily legislate on them. Should we be flooding Parliament with teachers before we vote on an education bill? With soldiers before we agree the defence budget? With owners of pit bull terriers before we vote on a law against dangerous dogs? MPs are elected to represent all their constituents, and can be voted out if they do not; ghettoising[52] our politics in this way is very divisive.

GOVERNMENT WHIP

On a point of information.[53]

LEADER OF THE OPPOSITION

Yes please.

GOVERNMENT WHIP

There is a fundamental difference between making Parliament representative of shifting interest groups and making it representative of humanity.[54, 55]

LEADER OF THE OPPOSITION

My point still stands. To undermine the principle of Parliament representing all the people is to undermine the basis of parliamentary democracy.[56]

Now to my first point. The fundamental principle of

48 This is the nub of any 'quotas' debate, in fact the point of clash (see Chapter 3). Is injustice best dealt with by collective action (the Government's case) or by individual agency (the Opposition's case)? Most of the subsidiary arguments stem from this fundamental clash.

49 Good to use numbers to itemise your argument in this way.

50 The Deputy Leader of the Opposition has already attacked the Prime Minister on this weak point, but there is no harm in reinforcing the attack, for tidy covering of all the points as much as anything else.

51 Useful to know who Margaret Thatcher was and what she was like.

52 Another example of the emotive use of language. 'Ghettoising' implicitly invokes 'ghettos', the areas of cities to which Jews were confined by the Nazis. Mentioning Hitler or the Nazis in a debate (unless the debate is specfically about the Nazis) is usually the mark of a loser, but as this is only an implicit hint the Leader of the Opposition can get away with it.

53 Making a POI at this stage is effectively rebutting rebuttal. This is (providing you're in unprotected time) perfectly acceptable, and in fact makes the debate more dynamic and fast moving.

54 The Government Whip has successfully (and very concisely) pointed out that the Leader of the Opposition is guilty of Logical Fallacy #11, the slippery slope, by suggesting that ensuring equal representation for a group that comprises 50% of people will inevitably lead to equal representation for much smaller groups, even though this has never been suggested by the Government. The Leader of the Opposition's use of humour with his reference to pit bull terriers now comes back to undermine him by making his extrapolation even more absurd.

Ending with the word 'humanity' adds to the emotional impact of this intervention, as it includes everyone present (even more than the Prime Minister's earlier reference to 'the British people') and because it has connotations of kindness (showing someone 'humanity' means treating them with kindness).

55 Notice how it's the Government Whip, the last speaker on the Government side, who makes this POI. She seems to be supporting the Prime Minister against attack, though she is in fact competing against the Prime Minister and her Deputy in the debate. Of course, the Prime Minister could have made this intervention herself, but she wasn't quite quick enough off the mark, so it's down to the Government Whip to get the credit from the judge for making this intervention on her behalf, while the Prime Minister loses face by not spotting the fallacy in time. One of the paradoxes of BP debating is that you can appear to be supporting someone while actually undermining them. Sooner or later you will realise that this happens quite a lot in life.

56 The Leader of the Opposition does not really rebut this POI, but simply reiterates his position, so I think we can say that the Government Whip has won this exchange.

parliamentary democracy is that people can elect whomsoever they choose to represent them. For the government to give instructions to voters, telling them what gender their MPs must be, undermines this principle. It is likely to make voters even more disenchanted with democracy, and to make them even more disengaged from it. It also sets a dangerous precedent for further intervention by the government in the democratic process,[57] once having broken with the basic principle of the freedom of voters to choose their own MPs.

This is not to say that the lack of equal representation for women in Parliament is not a problem. It is.[58] But a system of compulsory quotas is not the way to deal with it. There are better ways to encourage women into politics: educating girls in citizenship at school; celebrating the successes of women politicians; a policy of zero tolerance for sexism and sexual harassment across Parliament and across all political parties;[59] changing the absurd working hours of Parliament to make it more family-friendly, and more like a normal workplace.[60]

DEPUTY PRIME MINISTER

On a point of information.

LEADER OF THE OPPOSITION

Yes please.

DEPUTY PRIME MINISTER

All the measures you propose are excellent, and we fully support them[61]. They do not, however, do away with the need to make equal representation for women in Parliament mandatory.[62]

LEADER OF THE OPPOSITION

The mandatory nature of your proposed intervention undermines democracy; the measures we propose do not.[63]

To my last point. The Government claims their measure will tackle sexism in politics. In fact, it will make it worse. Why? To return to my earlier example of those women who, inspirationally, have recently reached positions of leadership as the heads of the Northern Irish, Scottish and British governments. No one can suggest for one moment that they only achieved this success because they are women. However, once we introduce a quota system for MPs, this accusation can be made against successful women politicians.

(CHAIR gives the four minute knock.)

57 This is hovering close to the 'slippery slope' fallacy, but the Leader of the Opposition, having been caught out once already, avoids it by making the threat of future difficulties vague and unspecific.

58 Accepting the Prime Minister's diagnosis of what is wrong with 'Now' is a subtle way of undermining her case; if you agree that there is a problem, she cannot gain credit for pointing out the problem. The Leader of the Opposition has, however, accepted the Government's language of 'equal representation.'

59 This identifies a problem arising from a male-dominated Parliament which the Prime Minister failed to spot. As the Leader of the Opposition has raised it first, no one on the Government side can take credit for raising it.

60 Line of attack #10 (see Chapter 6); there is a different, better solution to the problem.

61 Defusing the attempt to propose an alternative solution to the problem by accepting that solution, thereby taking away ownership of that solution from the Leader of the Opposition.

62 This POI brings the centre of gravity of the debate back to the proposal supported by the Government.

63 This swings the debate back to the main plank of the Opposition's argument. The Opposition has won this exchange. The response also uses antithesis (see Chapter 11), making the Opposition's approach seem better by comparison.

Their achievements will not be respected, because they will be seen as having been given to them because of their gender, not earned on account of their merit.[64] This lack of recognition for their having achieved their success through their own talents and efforts will undermine the careers of existing women politicians, and will deter aspirant women politicians.

So, because this measure undermines democracy, it will make a career in politics less rather than more attractive to women, and will create problems rather than solve them, it must not be passed.[65] Real success for women, achieved through real democratic processes, is the way to achieve real equality.[66, 67]

CHAIR

I thank the Leader of the Opposition for his fine speech, and call on the Deputy Prime Minister to reply on behalf of the Government.

DEPUTY PRIME MINISTER

Thank you, Madam Chair.

Parliament isn't just a body for passing laws. It is a mirror held up to society, where the people we elect to represent us reflect us back. And what do we see in this mirror? A world still dominated by men. Change what this body looks like, and we will change the way we see ourselves.[68] We believe that the measure we propose is no more than restoring Parliament to normality, by making it reflect the world as it actually is. I will be arguing for the benefits of this change. It will change the way women are perceived in society; it will encourage young women to achieve more highly; and it will help Britain to progress towards being a more civilised society.[69]

First, though, to respond to the Leader of the Opposition's speech.

He claims that the measure interferes with the right of voters to choose their own MPs. Yes, our measure will change the relationship between voters and their representatives; but it will change it for the better. How? Voters will now have the chance to vote not for one MP, but for two. They will have more choice. They could split their votes, for example voting for a Labour woman and a Conservative man; or they could vote for one candidate on the grounds of who will be the best representative for their constituency, and for the other on party grounds.

(CHAIR gives the knock for one minute)

Currently, local parties have an enormous amount of power. If you wish to vote Conservative, you have to accept the Conservative

64 This is one of the most commonly used (and most effective) arguments for the opposition in 'quotas' debates.

65 Returning to the initial signposting of the main arguments, expressed in a slightly different way. Don't be afraid of repetition; this kind of reinforcing helps to fix the argument in the judge's mind (see 'Signposting' in Chapter 3, The Basic Skills)

66 Anaphora and tricolon, repeating 'real' (implying that the Government's proposal is therefore false). Also, ending on a positive note. Opposition is by its very nature negative, so to be able to make your counter-proposal seem more positive than what is proposed by the Government is particularly clever.

67 This is a well structured speech by the Leader of the Opposition, not afraid of some repetition to reinforce points. Rebuttal is very thorough and precise, with the exception of the use of the 'slippery slope' fallacy. He uses classic 'anti-quota' arguments (interference with appropriate means of selection, undermining of success achieved by the group targeted by the measure) concisely and clearly. Like the Prime Minister, he wins one POI and loses the other. Like the Prime Minister, he has one weak argument. As the weak point is in his rebuttal rather than in his main argument, he has a slight edge over the Prime Minister.

68 In one sentence (using anaphora - 'change … change …') the Deputy Prime Minister encapsulates both the Action and the Then of the motion.

69 Crisp signposting of his arguments. The Prime Minister has already outlined these, but repetition is nothing to be afraid of.

candidate the local party chooses for you, man or woman (and it's more likely to be a man); under our measure, even if you were firmly loyal to one party, you would still have two different candidates to vote for. So voters' choice is increased, not decreased.[70]

He further claims that the equality it seems we both desire can be better achieved by other means. We support all those means to greater equality. They are good measures towards equality. But so is ours; why not have all these measures towards equality?[71]

He claims that it is somehow patronising and demeaning to 'help' women by ensuring they are represented equally in Parliament.[72] This measure is not about 'helping' women who do not deserve to be in Parliament. It is rather about restoring Parliament to its true representative function. You might as well say that the Great Reform Act of 1832, which changed the situation to one where cities of hundreds of thousands of people and villages of a few hundred returned the same number of MPs to one where constituencies were of equal size, was 'helping' voters in cities.[73] It was not; it was simply giving them fair representation.

Now to my points.

Parliament represents the British people. Except that it doesn't. A young woman - a woman of any age - looking at Parliament still sees it dominated by men. So, too, do young men. So, too, do men of all ages. This reinforces the notion for everyone that it is men who run society, and that women are in positions of power only by sufferance.

MEMBER OF THE OPPOSITION

On a point of information.

DEPUTY PRIME MINISTER

Yes please.

MEMBER OF THE OPPOSITION

The Government's measure will only add weight to the notion that women are in Parliament on sufferance, because they will be; they will be there not on merit, but because of a quota system.

DEPUTY PRIME MINISTER

They will not be there because of a quota system; they will be there because they have been elected.[74] And a Parliament with the same proportion of elected women members as the proportion of

70 This is a very effective piece of rebuttal, as it engages with the objection on principle to the proposed mechanism by expanding on the workings of the mechanism and showing that proper use of the mechanism can answer this objection. Also, it ends with a nice concise antithesis ('increase' vs 'decrease').

71 Accepting the other side's counter-proposal and simply adding it to the Government's proposal. Their counter-proposal loses its force when it is added to the Government's proposals, and then made better by having the Government's proposal added to it.

72 That isn't exactly what the Leader of the Opposition said. It is not a complete misrepresentation, though; it is fair tactics to present your opponents' views in the least flattering light.

73 As with the earlier example of Margaret Thatcher, it's handy to have a store of examples from history like this. It is not an exact analogy - no analogy is exact - but it is near enough to make the point, and to draw the debate back to the ground of 'fair representation', which is where the Government is strongest.

74 This sounds good, and is a nice example of antithesis. Unfortunately, it doesn't really answer the POI. Yes, the women MPs will not be in Parliament unless they are elected; however, it is not true to say they will not be there because of a quota system. They will be. The Deputy Prime Minister would be better off reiterating the Government's defence of the quota system.

women in the world will send the message that women are of equal importance in the world.

This brings me to my second point. An equal Parliament will send another message. It will send the message to girls and young women that they can be as powerful, as high achieving, as important as boys and men.[75] And this will change the way they see themselves and, ultimately, change society, as more women move into positions of power and influence not only in politics but also in business, in sport, in public services, throughout society.[76] To give an example. Over 11 million people watched England play in the semi-final of the Women's Football World Cup in the summer of 2019. Why? Because it was shown live on free to air TV; in other words, it was given equal representation with men's football. As a result, tens of thousands of girls have been encouraged to take up football and other kinds of sport. What the Lionesses have done for sport, our measure can do for the exercise of power.[77]

DEPUTY LEADER OF THE OPPOSITION

On a point of information.

DEPUTY PRIME MINISTER

Yes please.

DEPUTY LEADER OF THE OPPOSITION

You talk a lot about the importance of the way women are perceived, the importance of the messages we send, the importance of image. What about the importance of action?[78] It's not much consolation to a woman on low pay, returning to work earlier than she should after having a child because she is on a zero hours contract with no maternity benefits, suffering sexual harassment from her boss,[79] to know that privileged, middle class, educated MPs happen to be 50% female.[80]

DEPUTY PRIME MINISTER

An equal Parliament would be more likely to pass laws that tackled this kind of exploitation.[81]

(CHAIR gives the knock for four minutes.)

To my final point. What sort of country do we want to live in? One where one group dominates over another, or one where all sectors of society are equally represented? A British Parliament that is equal will send a message to the world that Britain is an equal society. The

75 Anaphora with a crescendo.

76 Good use of asyndeton.

77 A good analogy, as very vivid and memorable, but also relevant; the equal time given to women's sport is itself a kind of quota system closely analogous to the quota system proposed for Parliament. The rather vague assertion about the thousands of girls inspired to take up sport is hard to prove and may not be true, but it is likely enough to be worth making.

78 More anaphora ('importance … importance … importance …') but also antithesis, contrasting image with action, and doing so via erotema, a rhetorical question.

79 Enargia, painting a picture of life for the low paid woman.

80 This POI is essentially saying your Action is not dealing with something that's wrong with Now (see Chapter 6).

81 This makes some attempt to address the POI, but in quite a cursory way. The 'more likely' reveals a lack of certainty in the effectiveness of the equal parliament in dealing with these issues, and the Deputy Prime Minister doesn't address the point about the social and economic background of MPs and how this may cut them off from the concerns of poorer people. The Deputy Leader of the Opposition has won this point.

fact that many high profile people and celebrities have come out as gay has greatly helped gay people in wider society to be accepted for who they are; similarly, equality in our highest law making body will help the cause of equality everywhere.[82]

So, what have I shown you?[83]

I've shown you that an equal Parliament would change the way women are perceived, both by themselves and by men. It would encourage more women to rise higher in society, and would help to make Britain a more civilised, equal society generally. All these benefits are in addition to the benefits an equal Parliament would bring for policy and law making, as outlined by the Prime Minister. Equal democracy is an idea whose time has come.[84, 85]

CHAIR

I thank the Deputy Prime Minister for his fine speech, and now call on the Deputy Leader of the Opposition to second the case for her side.

DEPUTY LEADER OF THE OPPOSITION

Thank you, Madam Chair.

The Government claims to be solving a problem with its measure; it will in fact be creating more problems. It claims to be challenging sexist stereotypes; it will in fact be reinforcing them. It claims to be addressing inequality; it will in fact fail to address inequality, if not worsen it.[86] I will be showing how the proposed 'mega-constituencies' will not serve democracy, how a quota system is itself inherently sexist, and how the promotion of women MPs will only make matters worse for other minorities.[87]

First, to respond to the Deputy Prime Minister's speech.

He claims that Parliament does not reflect the world as it is, which is 50% female, and that this sends a negative message to young women. But the voting register does reflect the world as it is. Women have an equal right to vote, and an equal right to stand for Parliament, as men do. If they are not standing for Parliament at the moment, not being elected, it is not because the law stands in their way[88]. This is not Alabama in the 1960s, where the law stood in the way of equal rights for African-Americans.[89] This is Britain in the 21st century. Women can stand for Parliament; women can be Prime Minister, and two already have been. Yes, equal representation is desirable, but the way to achieve it is not through quotas, interfering with the democratic process, it is by encouraging young women to enter politics and to achieve success on their own merits; to reach

82 This keeps with the theme of his speech about image and perception, but doesn't add anything very substantial or new.

83 Hyphophora, asking and answering your own question; a good way to sum up a case.

84 Good to end with a rousing sound bite of a statement like this. Also broadening out the case from just 'equal parliament' to 'equal democracy', making it sound as if the entire system is being changed.

85 This is a well constructed speech by the Deputy Prime Minister. His initial rebuttal of the Leader of the Opposition's speech is very detailed and highly effective, not just dealing with the Opposition's arguments but moving forward and building on his own. However, his response to the two POIs is slight and a little evasive, not getting to grips with them thoroughly enough. Also, the substance of his speech, focusing more on appearance and image, lacks evidential weight.

86 Good use of anithesis, balancing what the Government claim will be achieved with what the actual outcome will be.

87 Good clear signposting of the arguments.

88 This is a central argument for the opposition in any 'quotas' debate; provided the law / system as it stands is fair, there is no reason to change it. In terms of the Now / Action / Then analysis we discussed in Chapter 6, they are saying there is no problem with Now.

89 A good example of using historical knowledge to make an analogy. It works emotionally, by evoking the horrors of racism.

the top in the confident knowledge that they did this for themselves.[90]

(CHAIR gives the knock for one minute.)

Now to my main points.

The Government proposes, as well as interfering with our choice of MPs, interfering with our constituencies. A constituency is a vital link between MPs and voters. Need a safe crossing near your children's school? Write to your MP. Fed up with anti-social behaviour in your local park? Call your MP. Facing eviction because your landlord has put up the rent again? Go and see your MP.[91] MPs have the influence, often at the highest level of government, to help their constituents, and they respond to these concerns and issues because they know, care about and frequently live in their constituency. However, it can be difficult enough already for MPs, particularly in rural constituencies with a wide area, to keep in touch with all the issues their constituency faces. Double the size of the constituency, as the Government proposes with its plan to create 'mega-constituencies',[92] and you double the size of the task for a conscientious MP. MPs will become even more remote and more detached from voters, leading to even more disillusion with and cynicism about politics.

GOVERNMENT WHIP

On a point of information.

DEPUTY LEADER OF THE OPPOSITION

Yes please.

GOVERNMENT WHIP

When we double the size of the constituency, we will also be doubling the size of the representation. Our measure will provide voters with not one MP to represent their interests, but two. A voter who wanted to approach their MP about a domestic violence or sexual harassment issue might prefer to approach the woman MP. Also, if a constituency returned MPs from two different parties, with differing views, a voter would be able to approach the MP who better reflected their own views.[93]

DEPUTY LEADER OF THE OPPOSITION

Thank you. You have raised an important problem with mega-constituencies, in addition to the extra workload they create for MPs. MPs are elected to represent their constituency. If you have

90 The other key argument for the opposition in a 'quotas' debate; quotas undermine the value of the achievement of those they are supposed to benefit. In other words, the Action makes Then worse than Now.

91 Good use of enargia, telling a selection of mini-stories illustrating the practical ways in which MPs help their constituents.

92 'Mega-constituencies' is the Opposition's own choice of language and, just as 'equal representation' made the Government's proposal seem natural and normal, 'mega-constituencies' makes it sound overwhelming and unwieldy.

93 This POI very cleverly both turns what the Opposition makes out to be a problem in their proposal into an advantage, and also introduces an added advantage to their proposal. It manages to land two blows in one POI.

two MPs with completely different points of view, how can they speak with one voice on behalf of their constituents? Having one Labour and one Conservative MP would be like having two Prime Ministers; no one would know where they stood.[94]

Now to my second point. The Government claims to be fighting sexism with its proposal. However, its proposal is in fact itself deeply sexist. Why? It is the political equivalent of men holding open doors for women; of men giving up seats on trains to able bodied women; of men insisting on paying for dinner on a date with a woman. These customs, now rightly seen as anachronistic and patronising, are predicated on the notion that women are somehow 'weaker' than men, and that they need help and support from men. The Government's proposal does the same thing. It implies that women can only reach positions of power if they are given a helping hand. In doing so, it paradoxically disempowers them, as it sends a message to young women seeking a career in politics that (despite the evidence of the two women Prime Ministers already elected) they can only reach the top with 'help'; moreover, women MPs elected in this way will never shake off the perception that 'they only got the job because they were a woman'.[95] Better by far to have a level playing field; then whatever goals women achieve will be due to their own talent and determination. The Deputy Prime Minister cites the achievement of the England women's football team; would that achievement not have been diminished if the game had been made easier for them by making the opposition's goal larger and theirs smaller?[96]

Finally, this measure claims to address the lack of representation of women in politics. But why should the underrepresentation of women take priority? What about the underrepresentation of black and ethnic minorities in Parliament? Or the underrepresentation of working class people? Although this measure would have the outcome that 50% of MPs would be women, it is highly likely that those women would be predominantly white and middle class. Already it is the case that more women than men go to university, but that black and ethnic minority people and people from economically disadvantaged backgrounds are greatly underrepresented at university, a far more serious problem. The Government's measure would replicate this problem in Parliament; black and ethnic minority and working class people would feel even more excluded seeing one group given special treatment while their needs are ignored. Inequality in society must be tackled it in all its aspects if we are to have a truly representative parliament.

94 This isn't a very good response to the POI. It uses a poor analogy; MPs are not like Prime Ministers, because their job is not to govern their constituents but to represent them, and this is better done if they represent a wider range of opinion. More importantly, the Deputy Leader of the Opposition fails to respond to the central point in the POI, that though the workload has been doubled for MPs, so have the number of MPs; this reveals a fundamental weakness in her argument.

95 Expanding here on the central 'anti-quota' argument, that quotas undermine the achievement of those they seek to benefit.

96 A quick thinking and witty analogy that makes another of the key 'anti-quota' arguments; that quotas aren't fair, that they are a kind of cheating.

MEMBER OF THE GOVERNMENT

On a point of information.

DEPUTY LEADER OF THE OPPOSITION

Yes please.

(CHAIR gives the knock for four minutes.)[97]

MEMBER OF THE GOVERNMENT

We agree wholeheartedly that black and ethnic minority and working class people are underrepresented in politics, and would support measures to give them more access. However this debate is not about those groups; it is about equal representation for women, and that is what we are discussing. That said, a side benefit of our measure is that it would make it easier to introduce similar measures for those groups.

DEPUTY LEADER OF THE OPPOSITION

My point was that equal representation for women in Parliament is not the highest priority; other groups are more disadvantaged.[98]

So, to sum up my arguments. The Government's measure is a bad idea for three reasons. It will fracture the valuable connection between MPs and their constituents; it is patronising and demeaning to women; and it is addressing the wrong problem. For all these reasons, it is ill advised, would do more harm than good, and should be opposed.[99, 100]

CHAIR

I thank the Deputy Leader of the Opposition for her fine speech and call on the Member of the Government to make her speech.

MEMBER OF THE GOVERNMENT

Thank you, Madam Chair.

My colleagues, the Prime Minister and the Deputy Prime Minister, have outlined the practicalities and the benefits of making 50% of MPs female very eloquently and clearly, and have shown how this measure will make Parliament both more representative and more effective. I will be explaining in more detail the benefits that this measure will bring in practice at a local, national and international level[101].

First, though, I would like to respond to the Deputy Leader of the

97 Even though we're into protected time here, the Member of the Government can still make her POI provided it began in non-protected time.

98 The Member of the Government undoubtedly wins this exchange. She points out very clearly that the Deputy Leader of the Opposition is guilty of Logical Fallacy #6, Introducing Irrelevant Issues, otherwise known as 'whataboutery' (see Chapter 7, Big Fat Fallacies). Even if she hadn't, the speaker would lose points for using this bad argument. The speaker then makes matters worse for herself by not rebutting the POI, but rather simply repeating her initial, badly argued point.

99 Good clear summary.

100 This is a mixed speech for the Deputy Leader of the Opposition. It is well structured and organised, and it makes very effectively the main 'anti-quota' arguments of unfairness and the diminishing of the achievement of those benefited. However, she fails almost completely to respond to the two POIs made to her, and also one of her arguments (introducing the irrelevant issue of other minority groups) is fundamentally flawed.

101 Even though the Member of the Government and the Government Whip are competing against the Prime Minister and the Deputy Prime Minister, they have to at least appear to support them. This is part of their role, and they will lose points if they do not fulfil it. They must accept the definition of the motion and the mechanism offered by the Government. However, it is the task of the Member of the Government (and the Member of the Opposition) to extend the arguments by finding a new angle. The Member of the Government does that here by focusing on wider benefits the Government measure will bring.

Opposition's speech. She claims that the larger constituencies we propose will create extra workload for MPs, and that they will make MPs less representative. On the first point, while the workload will be doubled, so will the number of MPs, so there is no increase in workload; on the second, voters will in fact be better represented, as it is possible, even likely, that MPs will represent a wider range of views.[102] She claims that a quota for MPs patronises women by 'helping' them. However, she overlooks the fact that women might actually need help, because they are the victims of an institutionalised sexism which has marginalised them and kept them from positions of power for centuries. Quotas based on gender aren't new.

(CHAIR gives the knock for one minute.)

For hundreds of years there has been a *de facto* quota system, allocating 100% (or very nearly) of positions of power to men. We aren't introducing a quota system; we're simply altering the existing quota system in the direction of justice.[103] She rightly raises the issue of the underrepresentation of women and black and ethnic minority people in Parliament. Rightly, but irrelevantly. As I have already pointed out, the motion we are discussing is about a quota for women MPs, and we need to focus only on this issue.[104]

Now to the benefits our measure will bring. First, the benefits of each constituency being represented by both a man and a woman. As my colleague the Government Whip[105] has already pointed out, it will mean that, finally, every woman in the country will have a woman representing her in Parliament. She might want to approach this woman MP about a personal matter, for example an issue of domestic violence, or discrimination or sexual harassment in the workplace, and would be able to do so in the knowledge that she would have an ally, someone who would understand her predicament - who might have been, or still be, in the same situation herself - and would therefore be better able to support and advise her. Or, she might want to lobby her MP about a wider, social issue affecting women, such as the gender pay gap or the tampon tax; again, she can be sure of having a sympathetic and supportive hearing. In this way, women will finally be properly represented, and Britain will finally be a truly representative democracy.[106]

LEADER OF THE OPPOSITION

On a point of information.

MEMBER OF THE GOVERNMENT

Yes please.

102 This is slightly repetitive of the rebuttal offered by the Government Whip, but it is no bad thing to reinforce the point in more detail. Don't be afraid of repetition.

103 This is one of the central arguments in 'quota' debates; that the current system appears fair but isn't, so intervention is needed to make it fair. In terms of Now / Action / Then, Now is wrong, our Action will take us to a better Then.

104 This is reiterating the POI the Member of the Government herself made. Again, don't be afraid of repetition; it reminds the judge of the value of your POI.

105 Sensible to name check your partner, to remind the judge about his excellent point.

106 Moving from specific examples to the general goal of a better Then.

LEADER OF THE OPPOSITION

Are you suggesting that men are incapable of representing women's interests?

MEMBER OF THE GOVERNMENT

I am not saying that. I am saying that women are more likely to represent women's interests better.[107] However, if a woman constituent felt that her interests were better represented by her male MP, there would of course be nothing to stop her from approaching her male MP; she would have the choice.[108]

Now, to the national benefits. My colleagues have already outlined how our measure would promote the involvement of women in politics by encouraging them to become MPs. I would go further.[109] It will not only increase the number of women who represent voters in Parliament. It will also, ultimately, increase the number of women who become ministers and Prime Ministers, the people in real positions of power, the people who make the decisions that determine what kind of country we live in. Ministers and Prime Ministers are chosen from MPs. It is therefore hardly surprising that, historically, there have been far fewer women Ministers and Prime Ministers, given that, historically, there have been far fewer women MPs. A Prime Minister choosing her or his ministers - even one who genuinely wants to lead an equal government, with equal numbers of women - will find it harder to do so, faced, as she or he would be now, with a parliament in which there are twice as many male MPs as women MPs, to achieve equality. Equalise the number of women MPs, and you equalise the chances of women achieving power.[110]

OPPOSITION WHIP

On a point of information.

MEMBER OF THE GOVERNMENT

Yes please.

OPPOSITION WHIP

Equal numbers in the workforce do not guarantee equal numbers in leadership. For example, primary school teachers are predominantly female, but head teachers in the primary sector are predominantly male.

107 Qualifying what she said to accept the point made in the POI, but without undermining her initial point.

108 Cleverly reminding us of another benefit of the dual-member constituency.

109 'I would go further' sums up very well the task of the Member of the Government / Member of the Opposition; accept and support what the first two speakers on your side have said, and then go on to make it better by adding something with an extension.

110 This anaphora neatly summarises how the Action will lead to the Then.

MEMBER OF THE GOVERNMENT

That is an excellent example of the way in which our society is systemically sexist, and why quotas are needed to address this systemic sexism. Perhaps an equal Parliament might pass legislation to ensure that 50% of head teachers are female?[111]

Now to the international benefits. Currently, there are no countries in the world with equal parliaments. Imagine if Britain were to have the first equal parliament in the world. What sort of message would that send, not just to the British people, but to the people of the world?

(CHAIR knocks for four mjnutes.)

How much more would we be respected in the world? How much easier would it be for us to take a lead on fighting sexism and inequality around the world? Our parliament, and our government, would have greater credibility worldwide. The British Parliament is traditionally known as the 'Mother of Parliaments', but up till now it hasn't had many members biologically capable of becoming mothers. If it was the first ever equal parliament, it would truly deserve to be called the Mother of All Parliaments.[112]

So, I have shown you that the measure the Government proposes is not only fairer and more effective; it will also make MPs more representative, bring more women into positions of power, and will boost Britain's standing in the world. Who could not wish to support such a measure?[113]

CHAIR

I thank the Member of the Government for her fine speech, and call on the Member of the Opposition to reply.

MEMBER OF THE OPPOSITION

Thank you, Madam Chair.

My colleagues on the Opposition have already shown how the Government's proposed measure is undemocratic, patronising and counter-productive. I think we on the Opposition need to go further, and reach out to the Government, and say how we agree with their diagnosis of the problem. Britain is a sexist society, and this needs changing. We agree on this.[114] However, where we disagree is regarding the solution that they propose. It is the wrong solution because it assumes that equal representation guarantees equal treatment; because it does not tackle the true roots of sexism in our society; and because it runs the risk of derailing the fight against sexism.[115]

111 This is a very adroit response to the POI, because it takes the substance of the point (even equal workplaces can be sexist) and turns it against the Opposition Whip (yes, I agree, and that is why we need a legislature that is more likely to take action against this institutional sexism). This is sometimes called the 'judo move', using your opponent's strength against them.

112 This isn't a particularly strong argument (it can be hard to avoid a sense of scraping the bottom of the barrel at this stage of the debate) and the joke at the end is a bit cheesy, but it makes a nice rhetorical flourish at the end of the speech.

113 The first argument in this speech is strong and well made; the second and third are a little lacking in substance and over-extended. However, the Member of the Government's real strength is in her handling of POIs; she deals with both brilliantly.

114 Agreeing (or rather, appearing to agree) with your opponents is always a good way to disarm them.

115 This is veering close to the Introducing Irrelevant Issues fallacy that the Deputy Leader of the Opposition fell into. However, it avoids it by accepting (at least partially) the Government's diagnosis of what is wrong with Now, and focusing on how the Opposition's Action is more likely to lead to the Then that both sides agree is desirable. By focusing on an alternative solution, rather than finding fault with the solution presented by the Government, the Member of the Opposition also cleverly distinguishes himself from the first half of his team.

First, though, to the speech from the Member of the Government. She says that women will be better represented if every constituency has a woman MP, and that women's issues will be better addressed. This is to fall into the sexist assumption that there are issues that only women can and should deal with. Why should a male MP not deal with an issue of discrimination or sexual harassment? Why should he not campaign against the gender pay gap? Can white people not fight racism? Can straight people not take a stand against homophobia?

(CHAIR knocks for one minute.)

What is needed is for both genders - for all people, in fact - to address sexism. Partitioning the task off to women diminishes the seriousness of the issue. She says that women are more likely to be promoted in a 50 / 50 parliament.[116] Does she imagine, though, that the mere presence of women in government will address the endemic sexism in society? Margaret Thatcher was at the top of government for eleven years. Did she eliminate sexism? Did she care about women who had not had the good fortune to marry a millionaire as she did? The Member of the Government claims that an equal parliament will increase our standing in the world. Will it, really, if our society continues to be systemically sexist? Will it not rather increase our reputation for hypocrisy, with a 50 / 50 parliament as mere window dressing while the deep structures of sexism continue?[117]

Now to my main points. Equal representation does not guarantee equal treatment. It is entirely possible to have a Parliament which is completely representative of our society in every respect, in terms of gender, race, sexuality and socio-economic background, but which still does not address inequality.

PRIME MINISTER

On a point of information.

MEMBER OF THE OPPOSITION

Yes please.

PRIME MINISTER

Would such a Parliament not be much more likely to address inequality than the current one?

MEMBER OF THE GOVERNMENT

Likely, perhaps, but not certain. The election of the US's first black

116 Use of language. 'Equal parliament' sounds fair, rational, normal; '50 / 50' sounds uncertain, unstable.

117 This is the nub of the Member of the Opposition's argument; the Government's measure is not intrinsically wrong, it just doesn't solve the problem it says it will solve.

president in 2008 clearly did not eliminate racism from American society. In fact, Obama's time in power may even have done some harm by lulling people into a false sense of security, making them imagine that the problem of race in the US had been solved; the upsurge of racist rhetoric and white supremacist violence in the US under President Trump has shown how dangerous that complacency was. My concern is that the Government's measure will give the impression that sexism has been eliminated, when it has not; and that this impression will actually prevent sexism from being tackled.[118]

Secondly, the Government's measure does not address the real roots of sexism in our society. As has already been pointed out, MPs tend to come from educated and prosperous backgrounds; this applies to female MPs no less than male MPs. But the real scandal of sexism is not female Oxbridge graduates who were educated at private schools not getting as many promotions as their male colleagues. The real scandal is working-class women in insecure employment as cleaners or carers, unable to support their families; poor, uneducated women suffering silently at the hands of violent partners, knowing that the police will not take their side; women driven by poverty into prostitution, at the mercy of brutal pimps and people traffickers.[119]

DEPUTY PRIME MINISTER

On a point of information.

MEMBER OF THE OPPOSITION

Yes please.

DEPUTY PRIME MINISTER

These issues are all real ones. They need addressing. An equal parliament is more likely to address them.

MEMBER OF THE OPPOSITION

An equal parliament in terms of gender, maybe; but an equal parliament dominated still by people who know nothing of the issues I have outlined, and are therefore likely to think that because they have an equal number of women MPs, they have solved the problems of sexism when they have not.

(CHAIR knocks for four minutes.)

To my last point. A 50 / 50 parliament might look like justice. But it will not achieve justice. It will allow those who wish to keep poor women, disadvantaged women, forgotten and marginalised women

118 **This is a bold but very effective response; essentially, it looks like you have solved the problem, but you haven't, and that makes the problem worse.**

119 **This enargia energises the debate by introducing a whole new class of issues which have not been presented in the debate so far, and allows the Member of the Opposition to change the direction of the debate in quite a striking and memorable way.**

in their place, to say, 'Look; you have equality; what more do you want?' It will distract and divert energy from the real struggle against sexism, which is rooted not in political but in economic structures. It will give the false impression that the problem has been solved when in fact it has merely been avoided.

So, we oppose this measure, not only because it will not work, but because it is an unnecessary distraction from the real issues. It will not achieve equal power for women; it will not tackle the roots of sexism; it will be a mere smokescreen, hiding the failure to tackle the real problem. It is the wrong solution to a real problem, and must be opposed.[120]

CHAIR

I thank the Member of the Opposition for his fine speech and call on the Government Whip to sum up the case for the Government side.

GOVERNMENT WHIP

Thank you, Madam Chair.

I will be summing up the Government's case for a law making it compulsory for 50% of MPs to be female. I will be showing how the current situation means that Parliament is not doing its job, because it is not representing the British people, how our measure will make it more representative, and how the increased number of women MPs will change not only politics for the better, but society as a whole for the better. I will be showing how the Opposition's claims that our measure is undemocratic, unnecessary and counter-productive are wrong, and how it will be part of the solution to the systemic sexism in our society to which they refer.[121]

First, though, to respond to the speech by the Member of the Opposition. He claims that equal representation does not lead to equal treatment. Well, I have news for him. Equal representation is part of equal treatment.[122] At the moment, women - not just the privileged elite he claims make up the majority of MPs, but women voters, in other words one half of the population - are not treated equally because they are not being represented equally.

He talks very movingly of the deep systemic sexism suffered by economically disadvantaged women, and says that our measure will distract from their struggles.

(CHAIR knocks for one minute.)

However, I think that he is falling into the error of letting the best be the enemy of the good. Just because correcting one injustice does

120 This is a very bold speech by the Member of the Opposition, which tackles the problem of the third speaker's need to find new material for an extension by taking a radically different approach from the first two speakers on his side, without directly contradicting them. He deals with both POIs with the same bold effectiveness.

121 The Government Whip concisely summarises the points of all three speakers so far, and also signposts how he will be rebutting the Opposition. It may seem a little repetitive, but this is inevitable to a degree in a Whip's speech; Whips must not introduce any new ideas. The trick is to present the ideas in a fresher, clearer, more concise way

122 This sentence is a brilliantly crisp summary of his case. If you can boil down your case to a single sentence or phrase, then do so.

not correct all injustices, it does not follow that the one injustice should not be corrected; especially when correcting that injustice, by ensuring that the legislature will now be inherently more sympathetic to the needs of women, is more likely to lead to other injustices being corrected.

Now to sum up our case.

Britain is supposed to be a representative democracy. However, our parliament is not representative; it gives the impression that two thirds of the population are male, and thus reveals the reality that two thirds of power is held by males. Our measure would correct this basic democratic deficit. It would not, as the Opposition claim, weaken the link between MPs and their constituents; it would strengthen that link because constituents would have not one but two MPs, one from each gender.[123] It would inspire more women to become involved in public life, not just as politicians, but in so many other fields; it would ensure that the issues that affect women's lives were properly addressed, and that legislation was passed to deal with these issues; and it would change the current noisy boys' playground atmosphere of the House of Commons into a more collaborative, more constructive, less confrontational environment. Fairer government and better government would be the result.

DEPUTY LEADER OF THE OPPOSITION

On a point of information.

GOVERNMENT WHIP

Yes please.

DEPUTY LEADER OF THE OPPOSITION

How is a democracy where the voters are told what kind of MPs they can elect fairer?

GOVERNMENT WHIP

They are already told what kind of MPs they can elect by members of their local party, often a small and very unrepresentative group, selecting candidates for their constituency, candidates who will be overwhelmingly male. Our measure will give them more choice by giving them more votes.[124]

Now, to the points of clash.

The Opposition claim - have just claimed - that our measure will reduce choice for voters. In fact, it will increase choice, by ensuring

123 Good to incorporate some rebuttal within the summary like this.

124 This is a good response to the POI, as it reiterates the point about having more votes, and also in-troduces an extra benefit of the measure proposed.

that every voter has the opportunity to vote for a man and a woman. They would keep choice narrow, by maintaining the status quo whereby candidates are overwhelmingly male; we will widen choice, by opening up the options for voters. They claim our measure is not necessary, because there are other ways of tackling systemic sexism. Yes, there are, and we support them. This debate is not about those measures. It is about a measure that will tackle an inherent injustice at the heart of power in this country. Just because there are other things that could be done, it does not mean that this thing should not be done. They claim our measure is a distraction from the struggle against sexism; we say it is a part of the struggle against sexism. The Opposition claim that women can, and indeed on occasion should be, just as confrontational as men; we say that if they act like men at their worst it is because they are operating in a world run by men at their worst. When women are released from the need to work on men's terms, it will be better for both men and women.

MEMBER OF THE OPPOSITION

On a point of information.

GOVERNMENT WHIP

Yes please.

MEMBER OF THE OPPOSITION

Isn't it rather naive to assume that as soon as you have equal numbers of men and women in an organisation, everyone starts behaving better?

GOVERNMENT WHIP

Not so naive as to assume that a fundamental imbalance of power has no effect on the way that people behave.[125]

The clearest clash of all between our points of view, and where I feel the Opposition are most mistaken, is in their view that our measure is counter-productive, because it will somehow be 'cheating'; women will not deserve, or be seen to deserve, their access to power because they have been 'helped' by our measure. 'Cheating' implies that the current system is fair. It is not. If it was fair, why would there not be the same proportion of women in Parliament as there are in the country? The fact that this is not the case is sufficient evidence, surely, that action needs to be taken. The Opposition say we are interfering with democracy; we say we are making democracy better,

125 Another good response to the POI; crisp and focused, and bringing the argument back to the Government's fundamental (and strong) point about the imbalance of power.

more democratic. They say any success women achieve under our measure will be somehow illegitimate; we say it will be one of the desirable outcomes of a fairer system.[126]

(CHAIR knocks for four minutes.)

So, we on the Government side set true representation against misrepresentation; a wide choice against a narrow choice; a world where women are empowered against a world where they are marginalised and ignored; a world where injustices against women are overcome against a world where they are left untouched. A world, in fact, where women are treated as what they are: one half of the human race.[127]

Sometimes the system is broken, and it needs fixing. Over a hundred years ago, women could not vote. Many defended that system as good enough, and claimed that attempts to interfere with it would make matters worse, much as the Opposition are doing with our measure. The system is still broken, and needs fixing. Our measure will fix it, and will make Britain a better, fairer place.[128]

CHAIR

I thank the Government Whip for his fine speech, and call on the Opposition Whip to conclude the debate by summing up the case for the Opposition.

OPPOSITION WHIP

Thank you, Madam Chair.

We on the Opposition side understand the good intentions with which this measure is put forward. However, we believe that it is fundamentally misguided. It intervenes in the democratic process in a way that undermines that process; it distracts energy from tackling the problem of sexism; it is the wrong solution to a real and deep problem; and, most of all, the use of quotas is a fundamentally flawed approach to addressing inequality.[129]

First, though, I will briefly address the Government Whip's speech. He says that the fact that two thirds of Parliament is male means that two thirds of power is held by males. However, he doesn't mention that one half of the electorate is female; women have equal voting rights, and an equal ability to stand for Parliament. He says that this system is not fair, but it evidently is. What he does not explain is how his side's policy of excluding people from standing for Parliament because of their gender is fair. Justice is not promoted by injustice.[130]

Now, to sum up our case.

126 **This is a very good example of how to address the 'points of clash'; set up what your opponents say on one side, and then what you say on the other, making sure that what you say sounds better. It is also very effective because it deals with the points of principle rather than more marginal issues.**

127 **Using antithesis to contrast the Now that is wrong with the Then that the Government's Action will bring.**

128 **This is a very effective Whip's speech. It sums up crisply, and also highlights the points of clash. There is no need to be concerned about its apparent repetitiveness; like a good teacher, the Gov-ernment Whip is reinforcing the Government's arguments in the Judge's mind by repeating them with a slightly different emphasis. The Government Whip also deals very well with the two POIs.**

129 **This is good signposting of the Opposition's case, but it would be even better if it included some rebuttal.**

Democracy is an imperfect system. It may sometimes throw up results we do not like. It does not necessarily result in a perfectly representative Parliament, precisely mirroring the people it is supposed to represent. However, it is fundamentally fair. Anyone can stand for election.

(CHAIR knocks for one minute)

One person (male or female), one vote. Whoever gets the most votes in a constituency, wins. It is clear, it is simple, and (I reiterate) it is fair. No matter how good the intentions, we interfere with this system at our peril. Once the precedent is set, there is scope for other, less savoury, tinkering with our electoral system, of the sort which excluded black people from exercising their voting rights in the South of the United States in the last century.

DEPUTY PRIME MINISTER

On a point of information.

OPPOSITION WHIP

Yes please.

DEPUTY PRIME MINISTER

You cannot equate measures promoting discrimination against people on grounds of their race with a measure promoting gender equality.

OPPOSITION WHIP

I am not doing that; I am not saying your measure is racist. I am simply pointing out the dangers of interfering with a free, open electoral system.[131]

The relationship between an MP and their voters is a precious part of our democratic system. We interfere with this, too, at our peril. MPs are held in low enough respect as it is; telling voters what sort of MP they should elect will only make this worse. So, too, will creating constituencies that are large and impersonal.

Yes, we do want more women in public life. That is a very desirable aim, which we share with the Government. But we want them to achieve this aim by encouragement and support, not by an artificial system which distorts and interferes with our democracy. We do want to address the real issues that affect women, such as domestic violence, insecure employment and sexual harassment; but playing a numbers game with MPs - most of whom are already very privileged - will not achieve this aim.[132]

130 Quite brief rebuttal, but this is appropriate for the Opposition Whip, given that the Government Whip will not have introduced any new ideas.

131 The Opposition Whip puts up a good defence, but the Prime Minister has exposed a flaw in her argument. The analogy is too extreme, and is also tending towards the Slippery Slope fallacy (see Chapter 7, Big Fat Fallacies); it's a long way from all-women voting lists to black people being turned away from polling stations.

132 This doesn't quite hit the spot as she doesn't say why the 'numbers game' won't work.

Above all, though, we reject the very concept of quotas. Quotas distort the systems they intervene in, and they undermine the people they claim to support. We heard much from the Government about the plight of an ambitious young woman, deterred from entering politics. How will this young woman feel if she achieves success not on her own merits, but as a statutory woman in a two person constituency? How, indeed, would a young man, eminently qualified to be a candidate, but excluded because of his gender, feel? How will this promote either self-respect or respect for women politicians?[133]

PRIME MINISTER

On a point of information.

OPPOSITION WHIP

Yes please.

PRIME MINISTER

Women MPs elected under our system will not be elected as 'statutory women'. They will be competing against a wide range of other candidates on an all-woman list. They will win, like their male counterparts, because they have earned more votes than any other candidate.

OPPOSITION WHIP

None the less, they will not be competing on a level playing field, because the all-woman list will not be open to men. It will not be a truly fair, open, equal contest.[134]

So, to the points of clash.

The Government claim that Parliament is not representative. We say that it is, because our current voting system is equal and fair. They say that their measure will promote respect for women in public life and in positions of power; we say it will have the opposite effect, as it will create resentment and will undermine women's achievement. They say it will help to address the problems women face; we say it will be a distraction from these problems, and will only give the illusion of having solved them.[135]

(CHAIR gives the knock for four minutes.)

Speakers on the Government side have good intentions, but they are naive. Their proposed measure will only make worse the problem it claims to solve, and will not address the real problems that will still exist. Let us not give up the seat of power to women; let us

133 This is a much more effective passage of rhetoric, as it uses erotema to bring home the human consequences of the measure.

134 This is an excellent response to the POI, as it introduces an unanswerable objection to the all-woman voting list; that it is excluding.

135 Good crisp use of antithesis to sum up the points of clash.

encourage them to ask for it. Let us not hold open the door for women; let us encourage them to push open the door themselves. Let us oppose this ill thought through and needless measure.[136]

CHAIR

I thank the Opposition Whip for her fine speech, and all the speakers for their contributions to what has been an impassioned and stimulating debate. I would now like to ask the Judge to give her feedback, and her verdict.

JUDGE

Thank you, Madam Chair.

Thank you, too, to all the debaters for such an intelligent, engaged and competitive debate. The standard was extremely high. In particular, I was impressed by the use of structure and signposting; all the speeches were very easy to follow. There were some really excellent arguments, and some combative points of information. Where there were weaker arguments, they were very effectively called out in rebuttal. The final result was very close.

Now to individual feedback. I will take the speakers in their teams.

First, the Prime Minister. The mechanism was very strong and well thought through. The structure and signposting was superb. She dealt very well with the first point of information, turning it back against the Opposition Whip. She was, however, less sure with the Deputy Leader of the Opposition's point of information. Her argument was based too much on generalisation, and she did not argue through thoroughly enough the way in which the measure would bring about a change in culture.

Next, to the Deputy Prime Minister. His rebuttal was excellent, very successfully turning the Leader of the Opposition's arguments against her. However, he was a little evasive with points of information, not engaging with them fully. I also felt his arguments were based a bit too much on a rather vague sense of how women might be perceived, without much basis in evidence.

To the next team. The Leader of the Opposition made a very strong and effective assault on the Prime Minister's generalisations about gender. He also focused very clearly and helpfully on the central clash of any quota debate; individual action against collective action. His arguments were strong, with the exception of the 'slippery slope' argument, which was quite rightly called out. He could also have followed through more thoroughly with the counter-measures to the Government's mechanism.

136 This is a rather underdeveloped speech by the Opposition Whip. It is telling that she does not use the full time. She tends to assert her arguments rather than develop them. To a degree this is inevitable at this stage of the debate, but even in a final Whip's speech there is scope for development and amplification. She does, however, deal with POIs well.

The Deputy Leader of the Opposition's speech was very well structured and organised. It was very well focused on the key argument against quotas, that they are not rational and / or fair. However, she was rather evasive on points of information; also, the introduction of the irrelevant issue of other minorities was an argument that could never stand.

Moving down the table. The Member of the Government had a very clear understanding of the task of her role, and the need to introduce new material. Unfortunately her second and third arguments were underdeveloped and lacking in substance. However, the way she dealt with points of information was exemplary; completely assured and effective.

Her partner the Government Whip was very clear and well organised. He focused very effectively on the point of clash, presenting it with great lucidity. He also dealt with the points of information with complete assurance. This was one of the strongest speeches in the debate.

To the last team. The Member of the Opposition's speech was the most exciting. He took a very bold and unusual swerve to the argument, which both unsettled the Government and made his team stand out ahead of the first two speakers on his side. He also dealt boldly and effectively with the points of information offered to him.

Finally, to the Opposition Whip. Her speech was very clearly structured and easy to follow, and focused very lucidly on the points of clash. She responded to points of information effectively. However, her arguments could have been more fully developed; she could have used the full time.

As I said, the debate was a very close one. Each team had its strengths and weaknesses and none stood out against the others. So, with only a small gap between the teams, my verdict is: in fourth place, Prime Minister and Deputy Prime Minister; in third place, Member of the Government and Government Whip; in second place, Leader of the Opposition and the Deputy Leader of the Opposition; and in first place, Member of the Opposition and Opposition Whip. Well done again to all debaters.

CHAIR

Thank you, Madam Judge; and thank you to all the debaters once again for such an excellent debate.

What have we learnt in this chapter?

1. What a good quality full BP debate looks and sounds like ☐
2. What judges look for ☐
3. How to identify strengths and weaknesses in a debate ☐

Do this before you read the next chapter

- Search up a film of a debate online. Pause it regularly and analyse it in the way I have analysed this one, either on your own or discussing in your club.

- Stage a debate in your club with your most experienced debaters and film it. Pause the film regularly and analyse it. Record your analysis as a voice over and use the video to train younger debaters.

CHAPTER 15

Onwards...

In this chapter we'll learn about how you can take debating forwards as either a teacher or a student.

Having read this far, you now know a great deal about debating. Time to put it into action!

This chapter has suggestions about how to establish and sustain a debating culture in your school, and also how to grow and develop as an individual debater. It's divided into two sections, one for teachers and one for students, though each is welcome to read the other's section.

For Teachers

How to set up a debating club

How to set up and run a debating club

So, you want to set up a debating club in your school.

Easy.

If you want to set up a cricket club, you need:

- A large open space of land
- Ground staff to look after it and to cultivate and roll the pitch in the middle
- Cricket kit
- Bats
- Pads
- Helmets
- Balls
- Good weather
- If possible, a pavilion and a scoreboard

If you want to set up a rowing club you need:

- A boat
- A boathouse to keep it in
- A river or other large open stretch of water

If you want to stage a musical you need:

- A theatre
- An orchestra
- Costumes
- Props
- Make up
- Someone to design, print and distribute the posters
- Someone to sell the tickets
- Refreshments for the interval

If you want to set up a debating club you need:

- A classroom, containing chairs and tables
- Paper
- Pencils

See what I mean?

One of the great strengths of debating is that it requires very few resources to run; debating is, as it were, a cheap date. The one resource it does require, however, is teachers' time which, as anyone who has ever worked in a school knows, is by far the most scarce resource. (A friend of mine recently retrained in mid life as an English teacher after years as a freelance journalist and composer. I asked him what was the most important thing he'd learnt in his first year. 'How to make a cup of tea faster,' he said.)

Debating is a cheap date

I hope by now, though, that you will have been persuaded that it is worth investing that time in debating. You should be able to ask for (and count on) support from senior leadership, perhaps even in granting you extra time. Debating is an increasingly valued activity in schools, for all the reasons I outlined in Chapter One. It has always been popular in the independent sector; a very welcome development in recent years has been its growth in the maintained sector. It aligns very well with the mandatory promotion in schools of British Values, particularly democracy and respect for the beliefs of others.

So, how to run your debating club?

Have an initial meeting where you test the level of interest, where you can scope what you can offer. Ideally, you want different clubs for different age levels. As a minimum, you should have one for Years 7 - 9 and one for Years 10 - 13; if you have capacity for more divisions, even better! Of course, this means more investment of precious staff time. If you can, recruit a colleague to run one of the clubs. Alternatively (and in many ways better) is to delegate the running of the Year 7 - 9 club to a Year 12 or 13 student. In my own school, I have for many years had a formal role of 'Debating Captains', a team of Year 12 and 13 students appointed to train younger students, along with other duties. In my experience, older students are flattered and highly motivated by being given this responsibility, which gives them valuable leadership experience (and looks great on UCAS ...). I have also found that older students are far more effective role models than teachers; when I am interviewing applicants to be Debating Captains and ask them how they came to be interested in debating, they invariably mention the inspirational impact of the Year 12 or 13 student who mentored them when they were younger.

Then, you need to book a room and a time. Make sure you have a regular time and venue that can be identified with debating. The lunch break is the traditional time for extra-curricular activities. It does ensure that students are all on site, though the time can also be quite pinched; you will be lucky to get more than half an hour. Scheduling the club for after school will give you more time, though may also make it harder to get students to stay. Some schools have particular periods of the week ring fenced for extension / enrichment activities, and you may be able to bag one of these slots. Whenever you schedule it, make sure it happens every week; once you lose the momentum, it can be hard to regain. Be prepared for a certain amount of horse trading in the staff room over clashes with sports, music and drama. As in any negotiation (particularly with people you have to see every day), you need to be willing to make some compromises; however, don't be afraid to stand your ground when you think it is important.

What to do in that time?

I would suggest alternating sessions between instruction and practice. For instruction, use this book! Get all students to buy a copy (or buy it for them, if you have a generous budget).

For instruction, use this book!

Students need to know how debating works; take them through Chapters 2, 4 and 8 of this book. They need to know the basic skills of debating; take them through Chapter 3 of this book. They need to know how to build a case, how to mount an opposition, and how to spot, avoid and challenge bad arguments; take them through Chapters 5,6 and 7. They need to know some of the big ideas and big issues, and some facts about the world; take them through Chapters 9 and 10. Study the model debate in Chapter 13 with them. Do the exercises I suggest at the end of each chapter. Obviously, adapt all this material to the age and experience level of your students, and find your own ways to use the material.

However, as every teacher knows, the best way to learn about how to do something is by doing it. As soon as possible, get the students debating. Also as soon as possible, set up some kind of competitive structure.

Students are highly motivated by competition, and it gives them much more investment in the activity. If the club runs at lunchtime, the best format for a competition is likely to be Mace (see Chapter 2), if necessary with shorter speeches, say five or even three minutes, to save time. If you have a whole hour, for example with an after school slot, BP can work well, though students do need to be quite confident to tackle this more demanding format. For either of these formats, you will need teams of two. Get students to choose their own teams (unless there are particularly difficult social dynamics in the group); they will work better with people they have chosen. Set up a 'leader board', with teams ranked according to their performance over the year: two points for a win, one for a tie; if they tie on points, position determined by total number of speaker points. Set up a page for the club on Google Classroom (or whichever social media app your school uses) and post the leader board on it, along with teaching materials and reminders about meetings. The advantage of the leader board system is that it is dynamic and constantly shifting. Teams have something invested in it until the end of the season, and are motivated to act on the feedback you give them and improve. To ensure a fair outcome, have a fixed number of debates scheduled for the year, with each team having the same number of debates (ideally each team debating against each other team at least once) and then award a trophy to the team which is top of the leader board at the end of the season.

Use the school's reward system - commendations, merits, house points, whatever you have - to recognise the contribution and commitment of debaters. If your school has a 'colours' system for recognising achievement in sport, negotiate to have it extended to debating.

Some schools focus exclusively on an elite half dozen debaters, drilling them ruthlessly to win competitions and fill the trophy cabinet with silverware. That has never been my approach; while debating is a competitive activity, and should be approached competitively, I believe in inclusivity, and I measure success by the number of students taking part.

That said, it is often the case that debating clubs tend to attract ambitious, gifted and talented students. The debating club can be an invaluable way for such students to meet and make friends with like minded students. In some cases, if they are in a school where it isn't cool to be clever, the club can be something of a refuge. Similarly, if your school is one where sporting success is highly valued, debating can provide an opportunity to shine at a competitive activity for students who do not enjoy sport.

Students are highly motivated by competition

Do whatever you can to build an *espirit de corps* in the club. Organise a cake rota for meetings. Get hoodies or T shirts printed, with a debating club logo. Have a club outing to the local pizza restaurant at the end of the year.

Keep a high profile for debating

If you can, take the competition outside the club to the wider school. Work within the school's existing structures as far as possible. Many schools have a house system, which is used for sports, drama and music competitions. Add debating to the list of competitions, preferably with a competition for each age group. This will greatly increase the interest in and visibility of debating. House leaders and members of the house will encourage students to take part, and will turn up to debates to support their house. If your school doesn't have a house system, or similar pastoral divisions, have students enter a school wide competition as self-chosen teams. Work towards a high profile final for each competition. Ideally, run a leader board system (see above) in order to sustain interest throughout the year, and stage the final between the top two teams. If you don't have time for this, run a 'knock-out' system. In this system, teams are drawn at random to compete against each other in rounds. After each round, the losing teams are eliminated, reducing the number of teams by half. Then another round is set up and run, eliminating another half of the teams, and so on until you have just two teams left, who compete in the final, the winning team being awarded the trophy.

Keep as high a profile as you can for debating within your school. If you can negotiate it, have a whole year group, or even Key Stage, off timetable to watch the debating finals. If your budget allows, invest in trophies for all the competitions, and get winners' names engraved on them. Have them presented in Assembly. Take photos of both internal and external competitions (see below) and post them in your school newsletter, on the school website, on the school social media feed, even in the local press. Senior leadership will appreciate the raising of the school's profile in this way, and will be motivated to support debating more.

External competitions

Even more motivating for students than internal competition is the opportunity to take part in external competitions. They do of course mean more teacher time, mostly in the evenings, in addition to the considerable amount of paperwork required whenever you take students out of school. However, the honour of representing the school and the excitement of travelling to other venues and meeting other students means a lot to students, and will greatly increase their loyalty to the club and to debating. It will hugely improve their debating skills, particularly if they find themselves up against more experienced debaters. External competitions also offer more opportunities for raising the profile of the debating club (especially if you win!).

Here is a survey of competitions:

English Speaking Union

The English Speaking Union (ESU) (www.esu.org) can fairly be described as the 'original and best' schools debating organisation in Britain. Founded in 1918 in the aftermath of the First World War, with the hope that encouraging effective communication between people would promote mutual understanding, it is a charity whose stated mission is 'to give young people the speaking and listening skills and the cross-cultural understanding they need to thrive.' Debating is a central part of their work. The ESU Mace competition has been running since 1957, and former winners include a number of high profile figures in politics and the media. It regularly attracts over 300 schools from across Britain and Ireland.

The format used in the competition is Mace (see Chapter 2, How Debating Works). It uses long prep, with motions released in advance. It is a good competition for beginners, as the long prep format means it is possible for teachers to offer students a lot of support in preparation, and because the Mace format tends to be slightly more formal and less spontaneous than BP, making it less intimidating for newcomers. Though there is no formal age limit, students taking part tend to be Year 10 and above, mostly Years 12 and 13.

External competition will raise your profile.

The competition is run on a knockout basis, starting in October / November with local rounds, proceeding to regional rounds covering larger and larger areas (e.g. West London, London, South East, England), culminating in the final in March at Dartmouth House, the magnificent Georgian house in Mayfair that the ESU has as its headquarters. All rounds but the final are hosted by schools. Volunteering to host a round means a certain amount of work setting up the round, but it does give your students home advantage (and also saves you all the paperwork involved in taking students out of school). Rounds are judged by ESU staff trained in how to judge debates, who will give detailed feedback (make sure students listen carefully to this, and act on it; it is one of the best ways for them to improve). The ESU offers a wide range of resources for teachers entering the competition on their website. There is an entrance fee, though that may be waived for schools with a large number of disadvantaged students. The knockout format does mean that, particularly for inexperienced schools, there is the risk of being eliminated early on and only getting one outing. However, the fact that the ESU is a well established institution with full time staff, and that the Mace has been running for so long, means that it is a very trustworthy, reliable and well organised competition.

The ESU also runs the London Debate Challenge. This is free of charge, and is open to Years 7 - 9 students at maintained schools in London. It starts in May, with local rounds which incorporate a training session for students before the competition begins. There is then one more round before the final at Dartmouth House in July. The format is Extended Mace and long prep.

The ESU is trustworthy, reliable and well organised

Oxford Union and Cambridge Union

These are the most high profile 'university' competitions. The Oxford Union (www.oxfordschools.net) and Cambridge Union (www.cambridgedebating.com) are the debating societies of Britain's two elite universities. Their main focus is on staging debates of their own, in which a vast array of often very high profile public figures take part. They are also famous for being a breeding ground for future political leaders, and an exceptionally high number of politicians and Prime Ministers have been Presidents of the Oxford or Cambridge Union during their student days.

The competitions they run for schools are BP and short prep. As with ESU, they start with local rounds, then progress to regional finals and to a national final, hosted in Oxford or Cambridge. They also offer training workshops. The main competition tends to be dominated by Years 12 and 13 students, but they also jointly offer (taking turns to host it) the International Competition for Young Debaters, for students in Year 10 and below, also BP and short prep. There is a fee for taking part in both competitions. Given the BP format, these are more challenging competitions and are better suited to more gifted and confident students.

For better or for worse, the Oxbridge 'brand' still has a huge amount of power in Britain, and there is quite a thrill for students in taking part, particularly if they make it to the Final and get to compete on the premises of the Oxford or Cambridge Unions. Both these buildings are Victorian Gothic in style, with cosy committee rooms, a well stocked library, and a debating chamber modelled on the House of Commons. A fun game is looking at all the photos on the walls and trying to spot current and past politicians when they were students. A lot of people you have heard of will be there.

The disadvantage of undergraduate-run competitions is that they are … run by undergraduates. Some years they work very hard and do an absolutely brilliant job. Some years, however, reminders are not sent out, emails go missing or are not replied to, judges turn up an hour late, attempts are made to organise a debate at very short notice with no understanding of the procedures schools have to go through. Undergraduates do not have the experience of how schools and children work that teachers have; nor do they necessarily have the administrative skills that are a vital part of any teacher's toolkit. Another disadvantage of undergraduate-led competitions is that there is much less of the 'institutional memory' that schools have, given that no one stays more than three years. There is also a slight sense with Oxford and Cambridge Union that members see schools competitions as a lesser priority than their main work of schmoozing high profile speakers at the Union in the hope of being equally famous themselves one day and / or scheming and conspiring to be the next President of the Union.

It is quite a thrill to compete at the Oxford or Cambridge Union

Having said all that, the undergraduates who run these competitions are phenomenally gifted debaters, who are used to competing at a very high level. This means that they have a huge amount of expertise, and their feedback to students will be, though challenging, very valuable for them.

Other university competitions

Many other university debating societies run debating competitions, though these are likely to be one day events on a weekend, without the national reach of the Oxford and Cambridge Union. They provide a more intense experience for students, which can be very stimulating for them (though it does mean you giving up part of your weekend to accompany them). Given that the whole event happens in one place on one day, the administration is a little more straightforward. The format will usually be BP and short prep, and the students taking part are likely to be Years 12 and 13. Search up your local universities' debating societies for details.

Noisy Classroom

The Noisy Classroom (www.noisyclassroom.com) is a relatively new entrant to the debating scene, set up in 2011. In association with PiXL, they run a national competition called 'Up for Debate' for students in maintained schools. It is aimed mainly at Year 9 students, though Years 7 and 8 are also welcome. Only PiXL schools can take part; ask senior leadership if yours is a PiXL school. There is a charge for this competition, but it does include CPD for teachers and access to online resources. Noisy Classroom also run a competition for primary school students, which is free of charge, though at the time of writing this is only available in London. They have many resources for teachers on their website free of charge.

Do it yourself

Do it yourself ...

It's worth considering setting up your own competition with schools in your area. While this does involve some administrative work, it has a lot of advantages. You don't have to pay a fee, you can run it how you like, and you can use it as a way to build links with local schools and other debating teachers.

If you're not sure which schools are in your area, the sports department's fixture list is a good starting point. If your school is already part of a network of schools such as an academy trust, use that network. If you teach at a maintained school, contact your local independent school (particularly if, like many independent schools, they already have an established debating tradition) and suggest collaborating with them; they may well be pleased to have the opportunity for some outreach work to provide evidence of public benefit, which they need to support their charitable status. If you teach at an independent school, contact your local maintained schools to set up the same arrangement in reverse. An independent-maintained partnership scheme can also extend to the independent school sending older students to train younger students at the maintained school; this can be very rewarding for both parties.

You can run the competition as one off, one day event, most likely at the end of the summer term after exams, with a leader board running through the day and winners announced at the end. Alternatively, you can set up a leader board system running over several evenings during the year, taking turns to host events.

Don't be afraid to launch these ventures, but don't be over ambitious either. It's always a good idea with competitions - with any new venture - to start small and then build up slowly. Test the water with some one off 'friendly' debates, and then start with a small number of schools. Four is plenty, and a nice number for a leader board competition, allowing students lots of debating opportunities. If it goes well, you will attract word of mouth interest, and can gradually grow from there.

Start small and build up slowly

External Training

If you read this book carefully, it will improve your debating, either as a student or a teacher. However, you may also want to bring in some external help. Here is a guide to what is available.

English Speaking Union

The ESU run a programme called 'Discover Your Voice', which offers one day (six hours) and half day (three hours) intensive training programmes in your school for groups of up to 24. They can be tailored to the skills, age and experience of your students, from KS3 to KS5, beginners to advanced. It also offers 'Discover Debating', a programme for Year 5 and 6 students. This offers an introduction to basic debating skills in a series of weekly one hour after school sessions, with the intention of kick starting debating in the school.

For a more intense training experience, the ESU run an annual Debate Academy, shortly after the end of the summer term. This is a residential course taking place over three or four days, featuring training sessions, lectures on relevant topics, show debates and the opportunity for students to take part in several debates a day. It is exciting, exhausting and inspirational.

ESU also offer CPD to teachers. They run a Public Speaking competition, which tests different skills to that of debating, but with a lot of overlap.

Intelligence Squared

Intelligence Squared (www.intelligencesquared.com) offer two day (non-residential) debating courses in London in the school holidays. They also run regular debates with high profile speakers on current controversial topics, which are often superbly entertaining and informative, and make a great outing for any debating club. These are almost always held in Central London.

Debate Mate

Debate Mate (www.debatemate.com) is a charity dedicated to using the teaching of debating skills to promote social mobility. They offer regular after school training sessions to schools with large numbers of disadvantaged students; see their website to find out if your school qualifies. Debate Mate also offer CPD to teachers.

Hiring an in house debating coach

Some schools hire a debating coach for their students, in the same way they might bring in a specialist hockey or cricket coach. These are usually graduate students or recent graduates who have been very involved in debating at university.

The advantage of using this kind of coach is that they will be immensely experienced and able debaters, and will be able to pass on a huge amount of expertise to students. The disadvantage is that they will not have the knowledge of how children learn or how schools are run that teachers have. Hiring a coach will not let you off the hook of running debating; you will still have to do all the administrative work of booking rooms, getting students to turn up to practice, negotiating availability of students with the rugby coach, making sure enough sandwiches are ordered for the break in the competition etc. I think this kind of training works best if you have a very ambitious and able cohort of debaters who are keen to win competitions and are eager to be stretched and challenged.

Ask me ...

I offer a wide range of training workshops for students and CPD for teachers. I also offer consultancy for teachers on how to set up and run debating in their schools. You can contact me via my website, www.debatingforeveryone.com.

You can contact me via my website, www.debatingforeveryone.com

For Students

How can you get better and better at debating?

Being a debater is not only about practising all the skills we have covered in this book. It is also, to a certain extent, a state of mind.

A truly great debater isn't only a debater when they're in the debating chamber. A truly great debater takes the outlook of a debater into wider life. This doesn't mean disagreeing with anything anyone ever says on principle (that won't make you popular). It means having an attitude to the world that is open, curious and intelligently critical.

Being a debater is a state of mind

How can you cultivate this attitude?

First of all, you need to be informed about the world and what is happening in it. Reading Chapter 10, What Debaters Need to Know About the World is a start, but the world is of course constantly changing, and you need to be constantly learning about it.

When I was at school, there were three TV channels and not many more radio stations. Television started in the afternoon and stopped at 11 pm (with the national anthem). News came from bulletins scheduled at fixed times in the day, and from hard copy newspapers printed overnight and delivered in the morning. If something really exceptional happened, programmes might be interrupted for a 'News Flash'. This happened about once every five years.

It's different now. It's a bit like food. In the early twentieth century, many people in Britain were made ill by not having enough food to eat. In the early twenty-first century, almost nobody in Britain does not have enough food to eat, but many people are made ill by only having bad food to eat. Rickets doesn't kill people any more; obesity related illnesses such as heart disease and diabetes do. So it is with information. There's no shortage of it, but it isn't all good, and if you consume the wrong sort it can damage the health of your understanding. So you need to be discriminating.

Social media is a wonderful invention for certain things. It is a superb tool for connecting people with like minded interests, for organising people, and for disseminating certain kinds of factual information. I'm not convinced that it is very useful for educating yourself about the world. There is a natural tendency for it to form into echo chambers of like minded people who simply reinforce one another's prejudices without being challenged. The brevity of the medium also means that it is very hard to develop arguments with the length and complexity necessary to understand them properly. The anonymity of the medium means that anyone can post anything, without having to take responsibility for its accuracy or fairness. Moreover, there is substantial evidence that social media can be manipulated in a very sophisticated way to distort the outcomes of popular votes or to spread malicious and false conspiracy theories.

The advantage of what is sometimes dismissively referred to as 'the mainstream media' is that it is more accountable, and more controlled. Anything printed in a newspaper or broadcast on a mainstream TV or radio channel will have been fact checked and edited. That does not mean, however, that they will be free of bias, and part of being a good debater is being able to detect and take into account that bias.

The advantage of 'the mainstream media' is that it is more controlled

TV and Radio

The BBC has consistently been criticised for many years from both left and right for being biased, which I think is a very good sign. It is not without its flaws, but I still believe it is up there with the NHS as one of the institutions of which British people should be most proud. It is mandated by law (as is the case for all TV and radio broadcasters in the UK) to be free of bias. The accuracy and impartiality of its journalism is generally of a very high standard. The *Today* programme on BBC Radio 4 and *Newsnight* on BBC 2 can both be highly recommended. Its website offers a lot of longer articles; its 'explainers' are great sources for researching debates. The BBC also broadcasts many excellent programmes on current affairs, some of which I recommend as podcasts (see below).

Sky News is very good for deeper analysis, as is Channel 4 News.

Newspapers and magazines

The most useful part is the opinion and editorial

The Guardian, *The Independent* (online only), *The Times* and *The Daily Telegraph* are the 'serious' newspapers. They will give you facts about what is happening in the world, though each with their own bias in the way they are presented. *The Guardian* and *The Independent* lean to the left, and *The Times* and the *Telegraph* to the right. In many ways the most useful part of these papers is the opinion and editorial section (known as op-ed for short) which will feature columns expressing opinions about issues in the news. The best of these are superb examples of how to build an argument persuasively - very useful for debaters. *The Financial Times* is the best researched and most accurate daily newspaper, but (as its name implies) focuses heavily on financial and business news.

Weekly magazines give a longer and more considered view, their writers having had more time to reflect on events. *The Economist* is phenomenally well researched, and covers not just Britain but the whole world. It doesn't have any gossip or celebrity stories, or any sport (unless it's about the economic impact of sport) but there is no better guide to the world; read it every week and you will be very well informed. The *New Statesman* and the *Spectator* offer a lot of thoughtful analysis, the *Statesman* from the left and the *Spectator* from the right. *The Week* offers a very useful selection from the major news stories and opinion pieces, providing a helpful summary of the issues. *Prospect* and *Standpoint* are both published monthly, so can take an even longer view, in more detailed, thoughtful essays, often deeply researched.

Podcasts

Podcasts are nearly all free and you can listen to them anywhere, any time. Like social media, they are unregulated, so you do need to be selective. Here are some recommendations.

The Briefing Room (BBC)

The Briefing Room steps back from opinion to give listeners the facts about current issues. The presenter, David Aaronovitch, interviews experts with a real endeavour to understand rather than to persuade. Debaters do have to persuade, of course, but they have to understand first.

Analysis (BBC)

Analysis is similar to *The Briefing Room*, but tends to look at less immediate, longer term issues. Like *The Briefing Room*, it consults experts and presents the facts, leaving you much better informed.

The Moral Maze (BBC)

The Moral Maze has a regular panel who cross examine experts on an issue that has been dominating the news that week, and then express their own views. I have some reservations about the format; the panel can be a bit too sure of their own views on topics which they didn't know much about a week ago, and it can get bit shouty. That said, the cut and thrust of the discussion is an excellent model for debaters.

Beyond the Red Line (BBC)

Beyond the Red Line is a sort of counter-balance to *The Moral Maze*. It takes two people who have diametrically opposed views on an issue, and gets them to listen to each other and consider why their opponent might think the way she or he does in the hope of finding some common ground. In some ways it's a kind of 'anti-debate', but the empathy and understanding of opposite points of view it cultivates are essential qualities for debaters.

The Long Read (Guardian)

This is an audio version of a regular feature in the *Guardian*. It offers in depth, thoroughly researched analysis of key issues.

Political Thinking (BBC)

Nick Robinson interviews prominent politicians. The longer format allows him to go into more detail than is possible on news programmes. Politicians tend to relax somewhat and come across as more human, not least because Robinson likes to talk to them about their backgrounds and what motivated them to go into politics.

Talking Politics

This is hosted by two Cambridge University professors, David Runciman and Helen Thompson. As you'd expect, it tends to be pretty high powered and academic. However, it's well worth making the effort to engage with what they say; they are exceptionally well informed, highly intelligent and very perceptive. They also offer a wider historical perspective, and keep a helpful distance from the hurly burly of everyday politics.

A good debater should be an avid reader

Books

A good debater should be an avid reader. Books, even more than newspapers and magazines, are produced in a considered and thoughtful way. Here are some recommendations of books every debater should read.

Aristotle, *The Art of Rhetoric*

As we learnt in Chapter 11, rhetoric was big business in Ancient Greece, and there was a vast array of what we would now call debate coaches plying their trade. Aristotle was the original and best. You'll have heard of him if you study Philosophy; he is one of the great philosophers. *The Art of Rhetoric* combines philosophical principles with practical advice about how to persuade. It suffers from repetition and irrelevance in places, but it's worth persevering; there is much for debaters to learn from here.

Aristotle was the original and best

Jonathan Coe, *Middle England*

The best sort of novels contain debates, even are debates, as different characters and different groups of people present different points of view and different responses to what is happening in the world. As in a debate, the reader watches and listens, and can make up her own mind about what she thinks. *Middle England* is that sort of novel. Opening in 2010 and ending in 2018, it spans a tumultuous eight years in British history from the point of view of Benjamin Trotter, a fifty something man from Birmingham, and his family and friends. As well as presenting the characters' ups and downs and ins and outs, the novel debates many of the major issues of recent years in Britain: identity politics; anxieties about immigration; the effects of austerity; the divide between the generations; the divide between London and the rest of England; and above all, looming over it all, Brexit. By the end of it, you will have a much clearer understanding of what has been happening in British politics and society over the last few years. You'll also have laughed a lot; it is very funny.

Martin Cohen, *Critical Thinking Skills for Dummies*

Critical thinking is a vital skill for debaters; the topics covered in Chapters 5, 6 and 7 were essentially critical thinking. The 'Dummies' brand is well known for offering accessible introductions to complex subjects, and this book is no exception. It is set out in a way that is easy to follow, with helpful interactive exercises, but it will also stretch and challenge the reader, helping to make their analysis and construction of arguments much sharper.

Philip Collins, *When They Go Low, We Go High*

Philip Collins used to be a speechwriter for Tony Blair, who was UK Prime Minister 1997 - 2007, winning three General Elections, so he knows a thing or two about how to persuade. In this book he takes a selection of some of the great speeches of history, from the ancient Athenian Pericles in 431BCE to Michelle Obama in 2016, and gives us a detailed analysis of how they work, breaking down their techniques in forensic detail. He's not afraid to give examples of how rhetorical techniques can be misused; Adolf Hitler is in there. He also has very important things to say about how important rhetoric and debate are for a healthy democracy. Highly recommended.

Lewis Iwu, *Words That Win*

Iwu was a schoolboy star, debating for one of the few maintained schools (so far) to win the ESU Mace competition, then being picked for the England team in the World Schools Debating Competition. Now he runs a consultancy offering training in the skills debating has taught him to business leaders and charities. *Words That Win* sets out to show how these skills can be put to use in the business world, but along the way offers a lot of really practical tips for debaters. It assumes quite a lot of knowledge and experience of debating, and is most useful for debaters who have already reached a high level of expertise.

Sam Leith, *You Talkin' To Me*

This is a brilliantly written, highly entertaining analysis of how persuasive language works, peppered with hundreds of helpful examples. It ranges from high culture to low culture, from Hitler to Homer Simpson, from Cicero to J-Lo. It is also extremely funny; his three page analysis of a song from the *South Park* movie had me laughing out loud.

Rhetoric and debate are vital for a healthy democracy

Debbie Newman, *The Noisy Classroom: Developing Debate and Critical Oracy in Schools*

This book is packed with practical suggestions for things to do in lessons, ranging from formal debates to easy to set up, quick fire activities which will get students engaging in debate and discussion. Debbie Newman shows how debating in the classroom does not have to be restricted to the humanities, but can extend to sciences and Maths as well. Highly recommended for teachers.

Pros and Cons, ed. Debbie Newman and Ben Woolgar

Now in its 19th edition, this a standard reference book for every debater. It lists the key arguments for and against all the major debate topics. It is regularly updated as new topics come on stream. Essential packing for all debate competitions, as you will be allowed to refer to it in prep time. Don't make the mistake, though, of thinking that having good arguments will be enough by itself for you to win the debate; what matters is how you use them. Still, this is an excellent book, and well worth reading between debates as well, as it will make you very well informed.

James O'Brien, *How To Be Right*

O'Brien is a rare thing; a liberal talk show host. In this book he demonstrates, with transcripts from his shows, how he takes on and dismantles racists, sexists, and homophobes. While I admire his stand against prejudice and ignorance, I have some issues with this book. As the title suggests, there is something rather self-righteous about O'Brien's tone, and he does seem to pick the least intelligent and least well informed callers. Moreover, the host of a talk show always gets the last word, so it is not really an equal contest. It is a bit like watching a Premier League team knock a League Two team out of the FA Cup; convincing, but not exactly impressive. That said, he does demonstrate formidable rebuttal skills, from which any debater can learn.

William Shakespeare, *Julius Caesar*

I know of no better treatment in drama or fiction of how politics actually works: the factions, the conspiring, the delicate courtship of potential allies, the insidious undermining of rivals, the conflict between high minded idealism and calculating pragmatism, the sheer emotion of it all. Most of all, though, Mark Antony's speech at Caesar's funeral is one of the best examples of persuasive rhetoric ever written; it is worth taking it apart line by line and word by word to see how it works.

Shakespeare's *Julius Caesar* tells you how politics works

And finally...

There's no better way of understanding how politics works than actually doing it. So do it.

Get involved in campaigns; go to meetings; join a political party; be an active citizen; make change happen. Use your debating skills to leave the world a better place than you found it.

Debating will change your life. Use it to change other people's lives, for the better.

You are the future!

Acknowledgments

Thank you to Dr Frances Ramsey for giving me sabbatical leave from Godolphin and Latymer School to write this book. Thank you to the English Speaking Union for all they've taught me about debating, and for the great work they do to broaden access to it. Thank you to Chris Hall - www.instagram.com/cocurriculardesign/ - for design and layout. Thank you to James Renshaw, text book author and editor, for expert editorial advice. Thank you to Flora Bailey and Avi Shah for advice on the constitution and the economy; any howlers which remain are my own. Thank you to Jean and Alice for love and support. Thank you, above all, to all the hundreds (thousands) of students and teachers I've done debating with over the last 20 years, for your inspirational passion and commitment. This book would not exist without you, and is for you.

It is better to debate a question without settling it than to settle a question without debating it.

Joseph Joubert

Printed in Great Britain
by Amazon

70570055R00119